The Secrets of God

Who God Is,

And How It Applies to You

By Samuel Angelito Mananquil

This book is dedicated to my Father in heaven. Everything I am, and do, is dedicated to Your glory.

Table of Contents

Prelude

God is love. Seems simple, doesn't it?

And, yet, it shocks me when I don't see this principle demonstrated in the body of Christ. Often, I see hate when Christians look at someone who isn't abiding by God's laws. The way many Christians condemn homosexuals is a good example. I see judgment when Christians spread gossip. I see leaders offending people, and yet preaching sermons on not being easily offended. But being a Christian doesn't mean any of these things. Being a Christian means sharing God's love.

What we need to see is that love is not an afterthought to God. Love is the seed that branches out to everything that God does. You cannot separate God from love, because He *is* love, and out of that love, comes everything He does. When examining the Word of God, we must first look through the eyes of the loving Father.

We do not serve a God who is angry at us, nor does He desire for us to become angry at others. Rather, we serve a God who is madly in love with us, whose sole intention for sending His Son was to save us, because He loves each one of us. He didn't wait for you to get it all together to send His Son, neither should we demand perfection when it comes sharing God's love with others.

We need to see God for who He truly is. We need to know whom we serve. We can't simply go by what our parents taught us, or what pastors, other Christians or the Church may have taught us. We must learn who God is for ourselves.

This book strives to help you understand who God really is, from a point of scripture, and from relationship. As we progress through this book, we will find that although we may never know *everything* about God, scripture reveals the nature and true character of our Father.

You will see God is not a homosexual hating, fist shaking, thunder in His hand god that we fear He might be. He is a god who loves. We will see a god who is sovereign, and in control of everything going on in your life, whether it be good, or bad. And we will see how He can and will turn every moment into something good.

It all relates back to love. He loves you too much to leave you where you're at, and yet He loves you just as you are. He loves you too much to let you live in fear. He loves you too much to let you keep living a life without knowing the true person of God. God doesn't want you to know Him from a distance anymore—He wants something more intimate. This book will give you a glimpse of how you can achieve this understanding.

Why is this book called *The Secrets of God*? This book contains truths that people don't seem to know, but they are not secrets. They are not complicated truths, but simple, easy truths. These truths will open your eyes to who God really is, and how His plan applies to you. Let's begin the journey.

Chapter 1: God is Love

He Gave Everything

For God so loved the world that He gave His only begotten Son, that whoever believes in Him should not perish but have everlasting life. (John 3:16)

God is love. Everything He does, is motivated by one thing: His love for you. He loved you so much that He gave everything He had, not holding anything back. He gave you something invaluable, something eternal. He gave you His only son.

This act cost God everything and it wasn't something easy for God. It wasn't a simple task, but He knew you and I were worth it. There was no hidden motive. There were no strings attached. His only motivation for everything He's done for you—past, present, and future—is His love for you.

Sometimes we get used to people doing good things for us, in exchange for something they'll need, either now, or in the future. That isn't how it works with God. When God sent His Son, it was an uneven exchange. Sin tipped the scales against us. But God's love outweighed the sin and flipped over the scale. His love for you, outweighs any sin that you may have in your life. Nothing could stop God from getting to you back then, and nothing will stop Him from getting to you now.

What do I mean?

You see, in the beginning, when God first created Adam, man had a perfect relationship with God. God and man walked the earth together, spoke together and were friends. However, when Adam, disobeyed the instructions of God, a divide was put in place—a change occurred in the once close relationship. Now, man was forced to consult priests to speak with God instead of being able to speak with Him directly. God didn't want this change, but Adam's sin changed the dynamic of the relationship.

Because of Adam, mankind didn't have the same access as Adam did in the beginning. Gone were the one-on-one talks God often had with Adam. Adam and Eve were cast out of the garden, shunned. Now, man was a sinful creature. He had to atone for his sins in some way with God, so something had to die, to atone for that sin. Sacrifices had to be made. Romans 6:23 says, "…the wages of sin is death." In other words, a price tag was now attached to sin.

Perfect, spotless, and without blemish, animals paid that price by being offered up by priests. These animals suffered the consequences for the sin of the owner. This solution was never intended to be a permanent solution, but it worked until God sent His Son to be offered up as that sacrifice instead many years later.

When God sent His Son, He sent the eternal solution. He did this so sin would no longer be a hindrance to our relationship with God, and so we wouldn't have to go to a burning hell. The punishment that should have been on us, had, instead, been put on God's Son (Isaiah 53:5). God's son, Jesus, took our place. Now, instead of eternal hell, we can experience eternal life by belief in God. Our relationship is restored. The days of separation came to an end. There is now no need for animal sacrifices to atone for our sins. The perfect sacrifice has been given; atonement has been made.

But someone had to pay the price for atonement, and it was God Himself. The price, was steep. He gave His ONLY son, for you, for me, showcasing to all of us, how much He loves us.

We didn't deserve this. We didn't earn it. But God doesn't give us things because we deserve them. He gave this ultimate sacrifice simply because He loves us. We are the center of His love; we are His passion. Even when we don't see anything valuable or worth saving—He sees something too valuable to be tossed away. He sees someone so precious—someone He doesn't want to live an eternity without. You see, we are valued by God, and we are covered by His love.

His Love Covers You

Also for Adam and his wife the LORD God made tunics of skin, and clothed them. (Genesis 3:21)

And above all things have fervent love for one another, for *"love will cover a multitude of sins."* (1 Peter 4:8)

We see in the beginning that the heart of God has always been to cover us with His love. What do I mean? While, yes, there were consequences because of Adam's disobedience, it doesn't mean that the heart of God was set on exposing or shaming His son. On the contrary, God was focused on covering Adam with His love.

When Adam saw that he was naked because of his sin, he covered himself with leaves, which were scratchy and uncomfortable. On the other hand, when God saw that Adam had tried to cover himself with leaves, God covered him with "clothes of skin." In other words, God clothed them in something comfortable—something better than what they made themselves. This demonstrates how good God is, and it helps show us the character of our Father.

God covered Adam because, despite Adam's sin, God loved him. Let's apply that to ourselves. When we fall, when we make mistakes, we can expect the same treatment. God won't treat you like you treat yourself, or like how others treat you when you fail. That doesn't mean God approves of our mistakes, but it does mean we are always going to have His love surrounding and covering us like a blanket.

Sometimes, however, like Adam, we're fearful and we hide from God. We're afraid He'll pull the covering away and expose us, leaving us naked, and putting us to shame. Perhaps that's why we sometimes avoid going to church, or even coming before God. We fear God will embarrass us in front of everyone. After all, maybe that's what we've experienced in the past with human interactions. However, let me assure you, that's not who God is. We don't have to be scared and hide from God.

Remember that God didn't have to ask where Adam was hiding. God knew that Adam had disobeyed His command about not eating from the tree of knowledge of good and evil (Genesis 2:17). And yet, despite the sin which had left Adam exposed, uncovered, God still wanted provide for his child. He still wanted to cover His son with His love.

Some of you are in that same position. You've made some bad mistakes, and made some poor choices. Maybe you've done some things you're ashamed of. You may think that now God is coming after you. That just like when a kid breaks the TV by pouring water on it, you're going to get punished for what you did. But don't be afraid. God does not want to punish you because of your mistakes (although yes, there are consequences to them). He's not coming after you because He's mad at you. He's coming after you to cover you with His love, to protect you.

So our response should not ever be to run away from God, or to hide. Our response should always be to open our hearts to God and His love, to come before Him even when we make mistakes. Let God cover you. It doesn't mean that God approves of our sin, but what God is saying, is that nothing can outreach God's ability to cover and protect. So let yourself be completely exposed before

Him, so He can clothe you with His grace. After all, His love is unconditional.

His Love is Unconditional

I will arise and go to my father, and will say to him, "Father, I have sinned against heaven and before you, and I am no longer worthy to be called your son. Make me like one of your hired servants." And he arose and came to his father. But when he was still a great way off, his father saw him and had compassion, and ran and fell on his neck and kissed him. And the son said to him, 'Father, I have sinned against heaven and in your sight, and am no longer worthy to be called your son.' But the father said to his servants, 'Bring out the best robe and put *it* on him, and put a ring on his hand and sandals on *his* feet. And bring the fatted calf here and kill *it,* and let us eat and be merry; for this my son was dead and is alive again; he was lost and is found.' And they began to be merry. (Luke 15:18-24)

The love of God has no conditions. This is demonstrated in the parable of the prodigal son in Luke 15. The father in the parable represents our heavenly Father's love towards us. His love for us cannot change, just like the father's love towards the prodigal son never changed.

There was not one time when the father stopped looking out to the horizon looking for his treasure to return to him. Even though he knew his son wasn't following moral standards with his life, that he was misusing what had been given to him, it didn't change how much the father loved his son. Nothing could change how he would receive his son when he would inevitably return.

When the son does return, we see that the father doesn't merely walk towards his son, or look at him with his head weighed down by disappointment. Instead, he runs towards his son, ready to embrace him in love and tenderness, and grace. He wouldn't shame his son, or cast him away from his house. Regardless of what the son had done with his life, the father would always welcome him back home.

Now let's try to apply this story to our own lives. Some of us are that son. Some of us have run away from the love and tenderness of God. We've said, "*My* will be done." We've done things that aren't right. We've made some bad decisions along the way. Maybe some of us have done things we feel can't be forgiven and now we're thinking that we can't come back to God.

Friend, you couldn't be farther from the truth. Scripture shows us here that if you take steps towards God, He will run towards you. All God is asking for is that you make a decision and start taking those steps towards Him. He wants you to know He's not going to punish you for your sins. He's not going to harm you for your mistakes. He's going to love you, embrace you, and cover you. He's going to lift you back up, and He's going to restore you. Your sins have been forgiven. Your Father is accepting you back home. Unconditionally.

The son in the parable didn't expect this kind of love. He expected to be taken in as a servant. Yet the father treated the son better than the son treated himself. He clothed him with unconditional love, and welcomed him back home as his son.

The same applies to you. Even though you may have strayed, when you choose to come back, God will welcome you back with open arms, receiving and accepting. He will embrace you, just like the father in the parable embraced his son. God's love for you has not changed. You cannot outrun His love.

Consider this scripture:

For I am persuaded that neither death nor life, nor angels nor principalities nor powers, nor things present nor things to come, nor height nor depth, nor any other created thing, shall be able to separate us from the love of God which is in Christ Jesus our Lord. (Romans 8:38-39)

Scripture uses the word "depth" here for a reason. Depth indicates a valley. In other words, the low parts of our life. You may be in a place like that right now. This may be the worst low you've ever been in. But let me tell you this—no valley is too low for God to find you. It doesn't matter if you put yourself in that valley because of your mistakes. It doesn't matter how you got to the valley that you may be in. Furthermore, whatever it is you may be doing that's wrong even right now, is still not enough to make God stop loving you. You are still on His mind and heart. Forever and always.

It's wrong to think that God only loves you at your "height," or when you're at your best. He doesn't just love you when you're going to church or living right. God's love is not based on your actions. He simply loves you—everything about you. If God ever had a weakness, it would be you. You are His soft spot. You're the one He doesn't want to live an eternity without, and He's loved you at all times, just like the father loved the son in Luke. There's nothing that you could ever do, to make God love you any less.

Let's look at one more example in Jesus.

Then Jesus said, "Father, forgive them, for they do not know what they do." And they divided His garments and cast lots. (Luke 23:34)

When Jesus was on the cross, going through the worst pain any man could ever experience, His mind was still on you. His mind was on the same people who were shouting to crucify Him, the same people with whom He spent three years healing and teaching. His love for them was unconditional.

God has his mind on you, regardless of what we may say or do. He's not going to wait until you believe in His name. He loves you right now, whether you have Him as your Lord and savior or not— whether you're cursing His name, or praising it.

Jesus could have said, "Father, strike these people down.

They've done too much." And I'm sure the Father would have listened. Instead, Jesus cried out for mercy, and for forgiveness, on our behalf.

If Jesus didn't want to punish the people then, he doesn't want to punish us now. Even though our sin put God's only Son on the cross, it was never going to make God love us any less, or make Him want to punish us. That's not His mindset. That's not His heart.

For further proof, we can look to what the book of Romans says.

But God demonstrates His own love toward us, in that while we were still sinners, Christ died for us. (Romans 5:8)

God gave the greatest gift of all while we were still doing wrong—"while we were yet sinners." God didn't wait until a certain condition was met. Unconditional means unconditional. It can't change. It can't shift. It's only pointed in one direction, and it's pointed towards you, just like it was pointed towards the prodigal son.

Think about this: Despite our sin, our past, our mistakes, God still sent the best that He had for me, and for you. He gave us everything, when we hadn't given Him anything. He covered us, and our sins, when we deserved to be exposed. He loved us, when we were at our most unlovable. That's who God is. That's how He loves.

Chapter 2: Loving People

Giving It Out

A new commandment I give to you, that you love one another; as I have loved you, that you also love one another. (John 13:34)

Now that we've established God's love for us, Christ tells us that this same love needs to be demonstrated towards others. The cross is made up of vertical and horizontal lines for a reason. We love God, because He first loved us (1 John 4:19), but also, we need to love everyone here on earth beside us. The nature of love in general, and of course the love of God, is not to be held in, but given.

And yet, instead of giving it out, we often chose to hold it in. Instead of covering with God's love, we expose. We would rather gossip instead of pray. Praying for someone shows that you love and care for that person. When we don't pray, we've failed to love.

Instead, we've chosen to put so much focus on being "deep" and prophetic, like saying things that sound holy, or acting like spiritual gurus, when God has never asked for that. We put so much emphasis on our personal holiness that we've become just like the Pharisees. We're so full of rules and regulations, that we've forgotten the most important thing, what really matters, is that we love one another. We've spent so much time bickering and gossiping in church, instead of covering like God has covered us. We've preached so often on not being offended, but we haven't said anything about not offending others. We've become callous and harsh to each other, instead of showing the same love that's been shown to us.

Why would anyone come to Christ if all they see is a church tearing itself down with their words and actions? Why would they come to a place where they don't see the love of God demonstrated?

We've spent so much time tearing each other down, that we've forgotten to love. This can't be the case any longer. Everyone needs the love of God. We can experience the love of God on a daily basis, but we also need to demonstrate the love to others, too.

It's time for an illustration. When people mistreat us, we need to love them. When they hurt us, we need to love them. When someone cuts us off on the freeway, we need to deeply intercede for wisdom on their behalf (I say this half-jokingly). In other words, we need to love those who don't deserve it. We need to love those who make fun of us for our beliefs, who mock Jesus. That's who Jesus loved

16

as He died on the cross. His words were, "Father, forgive them, for they do not know what they do" (Luke 23:34). If Jesus could love the same people who shouted for His death, we can do the same. The same love of God is inside of ourselves.

It can't stop there. We need to not just love those who mistreat us, but all the people who live in the world. We need to love those who we've rejected or condemned, such as the homosexual, the prostitute, the pregnant teen, and the homeless. We need to love those who have been cast away by others. We need to love those who don't treat us right, and those who say bad things about us. These people are the ones that need the most help, the most love. It's not the well who need a doctor, but the sick.

And yet, those are the same people who we've refused to love. They're the ones we've shut the door on. It's easier to call them "heathens" or "sinners" and move on, than to open up our arms and love them the way Jesus loved us. It's easier to say, "Father, strike these people down," than it is to say, "Father, forgive them, for they know not what they do." Loving one another isn't the easy thing to do, but it is what God *commands* that we do. It's time for the church, for us, the people of God, to open its doors, not just physically, but the doors of our hearts, so we can love those who don't do right. After all, as we'll see in the next section, love never fails.

Love Never Fails

Love never fails. But whether *there are* prophecies, they will fail; whether *there are* tongues, they will cease; whether *there is* knowledge, it will vanish away. (1 Corinthians 13:8)

If you truly want to see someone change, if you want a revolution in lives, it all starts with demonstrating the love of God to others. That's what God did for you. His love got you from where you were, to where you are now. Trust that His love will do the same for others.

The love of God is the only thing in the world that can't fail. So the question remains: Why do we try so many others things that we know won't work? Using judgement, fear, anger, and intimidation have all failed. So why haven't we used love, instead, when scripture clearly says it's the only thing that will always work?

We've used other methods for too long. When we preach at someone, throw scriptures at them or berate someone, it only pushes them away. On the other hand, the love of God produces different results. A kind word, a listening ear or a friendly smile can soften stony hearts. People will be drawn in, instead of feeling pushed out. Love changes the unchangeable. It works on the unworkable. It pursues. It chases. It doesn't stop. Love never fails.

This persistent, unstoppable love is what needs to be shared. It may not always be easy, but it is what's required of us. What do you think works best? Beating someone with our Bible scriptures? Pointing out every scripture that proves they're wrong? Or do you think listening to them, understanding where they're coming from, and having an appropriate response would work better?

When you take the road less traveled, when you love someone who seems unlovable, you will see a remarkable metamorphosis begin to take place. I've seen it firsthand. Being kind to a coworker who was rude, praying and interceding for him, led to a friendship. Forgiving another coworker who yelled at me over the phone and hung up on me, led to her seeing a demonstration of God's forgiveness, and His love. Real change occurs when there's love involved. You will see a genuine difference in people's lives when you love, not because you did something great, but because the love of God was demonstrated to a soul that needed it.

Our sinful, messed up world doesn't need another person saying that someone isn't good enough, or that they're doing wrong with their lives. People have heard that time and again. What people are really looking for is someone can love them, right where they are. Someone who will love them just as Jesus loved. Once a life has been touched by a love like that, it can never be the same. It touches a need that man has carried throughout time, and once it's been satiated, that man or woman can't live without it. And we prove we know God when we demonstrate it.

Do You Know God?

He who does not love does not know God, for God is love. (1 John 4:8)

Have you ever withheld love from someone who was truly difficult? Maybe you haven't experienced the true love of God. When you experience the love of God for yourself, when you see Him as He truly is, the only conclusion you'll be able to come away with is that God is love. And you will be able to share that love with others.

Now what do I mean by "knowing God"? And how can we, as

Christians, know who God truly is? We get to know God by relationship. And we develop that relationship by giving Him our heart, reading His Word, and spending time in His presence. It's all about seeing the heart of who He is. But until you see His heart, you'll find difficulty in loving someone else. You'll always see the flaws, and the mistakes, but you'll never see the true person behind the flaws. And if all you're demonstrating is judgment, condemnation, and anger, what do you think people are going to think about God? When people see all this they aren't going to see a God who loves them. Why? Because it hasn't been demonstrated in our lives.

This needs to change. We need to start backing up what we say by the way we live our lives. We need to demonstrate the love of God because we know who He is. And not just to the good people, or the ones who treat us right, but also to the ones who spit in our faces. We need to love those who speak poorly of us. That doesn't mean that if they're bad for our lives we must keep them in it, but it does mean that we can forgive them, love them, and move on from them.

Remember family, love does its best work when we love where no one else can, because that's what God did for us. That's what Jesus did as we beat him, ripped out His beard, spat in His face, when we ripped into His skin with bone and leather, and when we put nails into His palms on the cross.

We won't prove to the world that we know God by doing great ministry revivals, or by walking on water. The world will know that there is a God, that we know who God is, by us loving them when they're at their most unlovable; when it seems we should be doing everything else but love them, we still choose to love them.

That's what God did.

Now, we have to ask ourselves. Are we willing to take the same steps? Are we willing to take the hard road? Remember, what we do doesn't matter, if love isn't the driving force behind it.

Without Love

Though I speak with the tongues of men and of angels, but have not love, I have become sounding brass or a clanging cymbal. And though I have the gift of prophecy, and understand all mysteries and all knowledge, and though I have all faith, so that I could remove mountains, but have not love, I am nothing. And though I bestow all my goods to feed the poor, and though I give my body to be burned, but have not love, it profits me nothing. (1 Corinthians 13:1-3)

Unless love is the primary motivation behind what we do, what we do doesn't matter. What does it matter if you can preach the paint off the walls if you don't have love for the people you're preaching to? What good does it do if you know how to lift your hands in worship, but you don't know how to lift someone up when they fall? You could be the greatest theologian in the world, could have unraveled all the mysteries of the Bible, but if you don't have, or give, love, it doesn't mean anything. The works you do, the homeless you feed, won't mean anything to God if love isn't your primary motivation.

It was certainly God's motivation. John 3:16 clearly states it and we can't do anything for God, without the same heart.

And yet, we've still done things for God with other motivations. We've done things to please man, to look good in front of the pastor, or in front of the "right" people. We've spent so much time doing so that we've forgotten that we aren't doing what we do for man, but for God. Our heart hasn't been in the right place, and with God, it's always about the heart (1 Samuel 16:7).

Although you may be able to fool people with what you do on the outside, you can't fool God, who sees the inside. It's not about good works, it's about the heart that's behind it.

So we have to ask ourselves, what is truly in our heart? Is our focus on ourselves or is it on others? What motivates what we do? Self-promotion? Greed? Self-righteousness? Or are we trying to show God's love in all we do?

What scripture reveals is that God is love, and we need to follow the same pattern. Just as God gave, we give. Just as He forgave, we forgive. We are the demonstration of God's love that the world is looking for. People have heard enough talk. Let's show we know who God is with how we love them. I know it's not easy all the time—it can be difficult. But believe me, as you draw nearer to Him in relationship, you'll see who He is. And from that knowledge of His heart, and how much He loves you, you'll be able to love those who you weren't able to before, as His love fills your heart. And that love demonstrated will never fail, because God is love.

Chapter 3: No More Fear

Stop Scaring People

There is no fear in love; but perfect love casts out fear, because fear involves torment. But he who fears has not been made perfect in love. (1 John 4:18)

Some of you may have experience with someone who used fear to get you to do what they wanted you to do. You may remember feeling this grotesque pressure on your back, almost a panic if you didn't complete what you were asked to do. And if you didn't finish, you dreaded how your superior would respond. You constantly lived in a state of torment and panic.

How good is it to know, that we serve a God who does not operate this way? Contrary to popular belief, God uses love and free will to accomplish His purposes. He won't put you under that pressure, or under that fear. He will never subject you to "do it or else."

God will never use fear to manipulate you in any way, shape, or form. There is no fear in love because God is love. Since God is love, and His primary motivation behind sending His Son to die for us was love, then how can we think God would shift sides and use fear to torment us into doing His will? God won't use fear. It's not in His nature to do so.

We need to understand that we don't do what God says because we are afraid of the consequences, but we do so out of love for Him. We do so out of choice. Think of it this way: when you love someone, you would go above and beyond to complete a task for them. You would gladly work harder for someone who cares about you, then someone who is trying to manipulate you. Correct?

So now let's examine ourselves. If God, our Father, does not use fear, why would we use fear to try manipulate people into God's Kingdom or into doing His will?

We often use threats of a burning hell and eternal damnation in order to coerce people into the Kingdom of God. Telling a homosexual they're going to burn isn't going to save anybody. What we are doing with this logic is pushing them away from God instead of bringing them closer. God would never bend anyone's free will with fear. And it's not how He wants us to gather others to Him, either.

Remember that we can't turn hearts, but what we can do is be a beacon of His love, character, and nature. When people see you, let them see who God really is. Let them see the God that gives free will, not the God who takes away choice with fear. Let them see the God who liberates with love. He is looking to set people free, not hold them back. That's what He's shown to you. Don't let fear take away your, or anyone else's, freedom. Instead, extend your arms with love and mercy; give to others as has been given to you.

The Cure

Let's examine the scripture above from another perspective. Now that we've presented the problem of fear tactics, and the problem of fear itself, we have to ask ourselves, what's the solution to fear? What's the cure, the antidote? Is it faith? Is it charging in blindly with reckless abandonment? No. According to scripture, it's love. The cure that we're looking for, the antidote, is the love of God. Love seeks out all the fear you have, that you've held on to, in whatever nook and cranny it may be hiding in and casts it away.

Some of us have fear rooted deeply in our heart. We think that by living in fear, we're safe. We think perhaps that fear will stop us from doing bad things. But that's not how God operates. Why not? Because, as previously stated, God will not use fear to manipulate you in any way, shape, or form. We should never not do anything because of fear. Fear doesn't keep you safe, it will hold you back from where God wants to take you. It keeps you away from God.

For example, some of us keep away from God because we think He has lightning in His hands, and thunder at His fingertips. We think that God is just waiting for the right opportunity to lay waste to us. We run away from Him because we're scared of who He might be. Although people may say He's a loving God, what if we get to know Him, and we see that He's not? Maybe He is actually mad at me. Maybe He does want to punish me for all the wrong things I've done.

But those thoughts couldn't be farther from the truth. God's not mad at you. If anything, He's madly in love with you. He has too much love invested in you to ever be mad at you. Instead of seeing God's arms filled with thunder and lightning, see Him as He's demonstrated in scripture: with arms full of grace and compassion (Psalm 103:8). He always wants to lift you up, not push you down. When Jesus was on the cross, His arms spread from east to west which represented how much He loves each one of us. Why would God change sides and suddenly be mad at you?

That kind of distortion is just what fear does. Fear is irrational. It's false. It can't tell the truth. It cannot remain in your heart, and needs to be cast out by His love.

It may not be easy. Fear may be so deeply rooted in your life, that it almost becomes part of who you are. But the power fear has in your life is not greater than the love God has for you, and because God's love is greater, all fear will be cast away.

You've lived bound, for too long. It's time to be free of every single fear you may have by the power of God's love. Once again, however, the key is in relationship, in His love. As you draw nearer to Him, spend time with Him, and let His love fill your heart, fear will begin to be cast out. God's going through every door in your heart, and breaking its power over your life.

Even if you're bound by fear right now, get ready to be free. It doesn't matter how long fear has controlled your life, it can't stop God from breaking its power over you. It may not be easy, but if you just believe what God said, He's going to set you free from fear's power completely without fail. You'll never have fear influence your life again. You'll live a life of complete freedom, and it's all because there was something greater than fear, a cure, an antidote: His love.

Don't Live In Fear

For God has not given us a spirit of fear, but of power and of love and of a sound mind. (2 Timothy 1:7)

Once you give in to fear, you stop living. God doesn't want that. He doesn't want us to live afraid. God wants you to do what's in your heart in strength, without fear weakening you. He wants you to live lovingly, and to think with a clear mind.

Sometimes we're so afraid that we're going to make a mistake, that we don't do anything. We live life in a box, unable to move, living in so much fear that we're going to do something wrong, or that we might make a mistake. We do it to the point that we stagnate. But our God is the god of progression.

Scripture says to be anxious of nothing (Philippians 4:6). This life that God gave us is a gift, and we need to live this life in the abundance of joy. Instead of living mundane and dull lives, we can live adventurous lives. Remember, Jesus said that He came that you may live life, and that you may live it more abundantly (John 10:10).

We've let fear influence our lives for too long. Are we holding back because of fear? When we say things like, "Let me continue to take this into prayer," we have to ask ourselves if we're doing so out of genuinely seeking God's direction, or if it's because we're afraid to move forward. If God has spoken to us and told us to go, and we don't go, we're living in fear and disobedience.

Just to be clear, I understand seeking God and looking for direction. I'm not saying we can't do that. What I am saying is that since you have the mind of Christ (Philippians 2:5), you can think like Him. Not only that, remember that God ordered your steps to where you are now (Psalms 37:23), and He won't lead you astray. If God has told you to go, don't hesitate, go.

Don't live carrying a spirit of fear, masked behind your prayers. You don't have to wait for thunder from the heavens to give you instructions for every single little thing. Don't overcomplicate things. Pray, receive your answer, and then move forward in confidence.

God has offered us freedom from all influences of fear, and He gave us something wonderful in its place; a spirit of power, love, and a sound mind. Don't be afraid to take the leap forward if fear is the only thing holding you back. Trust that God led you to where you are on purpose, take His hand, and jump. Don't stay in the same place for another minute. Go forward. Go where God has told you to go. Don't fear. Take a risk. Live adventurously. He's with you.

Fear Not, He's With You

Fear not, for I am with you; be not dismayed, for I am your God. I will strengthen you, Yes, I will help you, I will uphold you with My righteous right hand.' (Isaiah 41:10)

Perhaps one of the biggest reasons we don't move forward is because we think God isn't with us. We think, "No, that can't be right, it's impossible that's what God wants for me. It's too good, too big, just not for me." But that's exactly what God wants for you. He wants to give you His best. Don't turn away from it—go towards it.

Some of you may ask yourself, "Am I sure that's the direction that God wants to take me? It looks too hard. There's too much adversity. It looks too tough." Don't run! Move forward. God is always with you. He's strengthening you. There may be some giants in your

How was your experience?

Tell us about your visit today and you could win 1 of 5 $1000 Walmart gift cards or 1 of 750 $100 Walmart gift cards.

Díganos acerca de su visita a Walmart hoy y usted podría ganar una de las 5 tarjetas de regalo de Walmart de $1000 o una de las 750 tarjetas de regalo de Walmart de $100.

http://www.survey.walmart.com

No purchase necessary. Must be 18 or older and a legal resident of the 50 US, DC, or PR to enter. To enter without purchase and for official rules, visit www.entry.survey.walmart.com.

Sweepstakes period ends on the date outlined in the official rules. Survey must be taken within ONE week of today. Void where prohibited.

THANK YOU

How was your experience?

Tell us about your visit today and you could win 1 of 5 $1000 Walmart gift cards or 1 of 750 $100 Walmart gift cards.

Díganos acerca de su visita a Walmart hoy y usted podría ganar una de las 5 tarjetas de regalo de Walmart de $1000 o una de las 750 tarjetas de regalo de Walmart de $100.

http://www.survey.walmart.com

No purchase necessary. Must be 18 or older and a legal resident of the 50 US, DC, or PR to enter. To enter

Walmart >'<

NEIGHBORHOOD MARKET
408-556-4505 Mgr:HARIS
4080 STEVENS CREEK BLVD
SAN JOSE, CA 95129
ST# 02486 OP# 009043 TE# 43 TR# 02720

ACTIVITY TC	003993887727	1.98 X
ACTIVITY TC	003993887727	1.98 X
OVAL PLATE	003993887654	1.98 T
OVAL PLATE	003993887654	1.98 T
OVAL PLATE	003993887653	1.98 X
DRUMSTICK	007255411174 F	6.97 O
B J PINT	007684010132 F	4.38 O
HAAGEN DAZS	007457069400 F	3.50 O
	SUBTOTAL	24.75
TAX 1 9.375 %		0.93
	TOTAL	25.68
	VISA TEND	25.68

VISA CREDIT   **** **** **** 5933 I 0
APPROVAL # 473142
REF # 131100720081
TRANS ID - 461311184891740
VALIDATION - C25P
PAYMENT SERVICE - E
AID A0000000031010
AAC BD7F82395308351F
TERMINAL # SC010080
      11/06/21   22:08:13
              CHANGE DUE   0.00
         # ITEMS SOLD 8
   TC# 1113 0831 5706 6731 95

|||||||||||||||||||||||||

Low Prices You Can Trust. Every Day.
      11/06/21   22:08:13
      CUSTOMER COPY

way, or perhaps armies that are against you, but because God is the god of the impossible, everything you face you will overcome. Not because you're great, but because He's with you.

Sometimes, however, we act as though the lie from the pit of hell is truth, instead of the promise of God. We'd rather believe that God is against us instead of for us. If you keep thinking that way, living that way, you'll live a life of mediocrity. You'll run away from every good opportunity that comes your way, not because God hasn't blessed you, but because you've turned your back on it.

People in the Bible weren't successful because they turned their back on God and His Word. They were successful because they accepted God at His Word, trusted that God was with them, and went forward in His strength. They knew in their hearts, that if God was for them, who could be against them?

This is demonstrated in the story of Moses. Moses was tasked to deliver the people of Israel from slavery in Egypt, the greatest nation of its time. He was given an impossible task, and he knew it. He questioned his own ability, and repeatedly made excuses as to why he couldn't do it (Exodus 4). And yet, for all of Moses' concern and fears, we see him move forward anyways and do the impossible, not because he was great, but because of who was with him.

We see him as the instrument that God used to plague the Egyptians until Pharaoh let the Israelites go. Water turned into blood. Frogs, lice, and flies overtook the land. Livestock was diseased. Boils broke out in man and beast. Hail mixed with fire fell down from the sky upon the Egyptians. Locusts swarmed. Darkness covered everything. The first born of every Egyptian died (Exodus 7-11). Impossible things were done on behalf of God's people, because God was with Moses.

The same applies to you and me. God is with you, just like He was with Moses. It's not about you being qualified. It's not about your strength. It's about God's. You are qualified; you are able because God is your qualification. You will succeed in what He has commanded you to do not because you're great, but because He's with you. It's not because you're strong, but because He's strong. You too, can do impossible things because the God of impossible is living inside of you.

Now let's consider King David. He was not always a king. He was once just a boy who volunteered to face a giant, the best of the best, a well-seasoned soldier. Goliath towered over all other soldiers making it seem impossible to defeat him. The Israelites certainly thought so. They were tormented by him for forty days because of their fear.

Then some fifteen-year-old kid comes along and says, "No" to the same fear. Although it seemed the odds were stacked against David—he didn't care. He knew who was on his side (1 Samuel 17:46). He saw the same towering giant that had caused the Israelites to cower in fear, but his response is what set him apart. He didn't listen to fear. He faced the problem, with God's strength in his arsenal, and he moved forward.

You need to do the same. Whatever fear you may be feeling, it hasn't come from God. Whatever giant is making you cower in fear, should, instead, be faced head on. You will overcome the giant, no matter how big or strong it is, because God is with you and He is greater than the enemy that is against you. You can defeat anything that comes your way with God's help. But unless you face it, you'll never be able to defeat it. Remember, the armor of God has no armor for your back (Ephesians 6:10-18). That's because you aren't expected to run away from your adversity. You are created to face it.

We see this demonstrated in Joshua, Caleb and the ten other spies. For those who don't know the story, the summary is that the Israelites, fresh from roaming the wilderness for forty years, had finally reached the land God had promised them. They were at the end of their journey, and twelve spies were sent out to scout the land. What the ten spies saw differed from what Joshua and Caleb saw.

But Joshua the son of Nun and Caleb the son of Jephunneh, *who were* among those who had spied out the land, tore their clothes; and they spoke to all the congregation of the children of Israel, saying: "The land we passed through to spy out *is* an exceedingly good land. If the LORD delights in us, then He will bring us into this land and give it to us, 'a land which flows with milk and honey.' Only do not rebel against the LORD, nor fear the people of the land, for they *are* our bread; their protection has departed from them, and the LORD *is* with us. Do not fear them." (Numbers 14:6-9)

The Israelites faced the greatest adversity right before their promise was to be fulfilled. Yet ten spies saw only problems. Ten spies reported in fear because they feared the impossible. They saw something that was bigger than they thought they could ever be. They forgot the promises God gave them. They forgot that the whole reason they were in the wilderness was to get to the promised land. They forgot the great miracles God had done in the wilderness for His people. They didn't think God could do *just one more* miracle for His people. They were at the end of the journey and they simply wanted to quit. They wanted to run away. What a shame. They were right there, but they took their eyes off God.

However, two spies—Joshua and Caleb—saw God. They saw the same adversity, but they never took their eyes off God. They never considered that God wasn't with them. They didn't choose to be influenced by fear. When they saw that promised land overflowing with milk and honey, they saw what belonged to them, and knew God had been faithful to His promise. They knew that no matter how big the challenge, there was no way God would not fulfill His promise. They knew that God was with them.

These two men were among the select few that saw the dream God had guaranteed come to pass and they entered the promised land. Those who didn't believe, however, suffered a different fate.

All those who had done wrong by God were denied entrance into the promised land. They saw the beauty of the promise, they were so close they could taste it, but then it was gone. When they tried to take over the promised land anyway, they were slaughtered. They lost what was promised, not because God took it back, but because they chose fear instead of God. What happened to the ten spies? Struck down by a plague. It didn't have to be that way. They could have all gone if they hadn't lived in fear.

And yet, this can be such a perfect representation of us. We've lived in fear. We haven't trusted God would take care of us, that He would be with us. Worst of all, we have been guilty of taking our eyes off God, and staring, instead, at our own problems, our own giants. We don't believe that God is greater than our troubles, so we miss out on the fulfillment of the promise. We miss out on God's best because of fear.

Let's not let fear stop us anymore. Fear only has negative consequences, which is why it can't be in our lives. It will only take you away from where God wants to take you. It can never be used to influence anyone, and it can never influence you. The term, "Fear not" is used many, many times in the Bible for a reason. It's because God is with us. There is nothing to fear because nothing is greater than our God.

Will you obey today? Will you walk into your promise? What's greater in your life? Fear? Or God? The choice is yours.

Chapter 4: Judgment and Condemnation

Drop the Stones

But Jesus went to the Mount of Olives. Now early in the morning He came again into the temple, and all the people came to Him; and He sat down and taught them. Then the scribes and Pharisees brought to Him a woman caught in adultery. And when they had set her in the midst, they said to Him, "Teacher, this woman was caught in adultery, in the very act. Now Moses, in the law, commanded us that such should be stoned. But what do You say?" This they said, testing Him, that they might have *something* of which to accuse Him. But Jesus stooped down and wrote on the ground with *His* finger, as though He did not hear. So when they continued asking Him, He raised Himself up and said to them, "He who is without sin among you, let him throw a stone at her first." And again He stooped down and wrote on the ground. Then those who heard *it,* being convicted by *their* conscience, went out one by one, beginning with the oldest *even* to the last. And Jesus was left alone, and the woman standing in the midst. When Jesus had raised Himself up and saw no one but the woman, He said to her, "Woman, where are those accusers of yours? Has no one condemned you?" She said, "No one,

Lord." And Jesus said to her, "Neither do I condemn you; go and sin no more." (John 8:1-11)

By law, the woman in this verse deserved to be stoned. She had met all the requirements for it. However, contrary to popular demand, she was given life, she was shown grace, and she was given another chance. The only one who had the right to sentence her, sentenced her to mercy instead of condemnation. He didn't reach for the stones. He offered grace.

What does this scripture show us about God? When people fall into sin, or make mistakes, God doesn't wish to punish them or kick them when they're down. He's not looking to drop stones on their head. He's looking to lift them back up, to give them grace, and to give them another chance. He's looking to point them in the right direction. Why? Because He loves us, and because our price has been paid.

Remember the punishment that was supposed to be on the woman, that was supposed to be ours, instead went on Jesus at the cross of Calvary. There's no reason for there to be punishment for our sins, for our mistakes, when our punishment has already been taken care of. Jesus took her pain; He took her death. And He took ours. We now have the opportunity to get up from our mistakes without being stoned, and go and sin no more.

And yet, we have to ask ourselves why do we try to punish people for a price that's already been paid? Why do we do what the scribes and Pharisees wanted to do? Why do we try to act like judge, jury, and executioner? Why don't we extend the same grace and mercy that Jesus has demonstrated to us instead of reaching for the stones?

What stones am I referring to?

I'm referring to the stones we pick up every time we gossip about someone who has made a mistake. I'm talking about the stones we pick up every time we see a pastor, or a worship leader fall. I'm talking about the stones we pick up when we say that some horrible event happened as punishment for how people have been living their lives. I'm talking about the stones we lift up when we look through judgmental eyes. It's time for these stones to fall to the ground.

Consider this: Jesus, the only perfect one, chose not to stone this woman. What makes us think that we, imperfect people, can do what

Jesus chose not to?

We can't let this continue in the body of Christ. The Church needs to be a place where we can be open about our faults and failures without fear of being judged or condemned. It needs to be a place where people aren't fearful about being openly broken because they're afraid they'll be stoned. It needs to be a place where the broken can be healed, and where the ones who have never experienced grace before in their lives, can experience it. It needs to be a place, where people who don't know God, will see His love demonstrated.

But we've misrepresented Him too often. We've stoned people—maybe not literally, but with our words and our judgements. We stone because it's easier to stone than to lift up that person. As a result, people can't receive healing, and they are hurt instead. Do you truly think that stoning people, judging, is what God wants His people to do? Do you think those actions truly reveal who God is?

It doesn't. Scripture here clearly reveals the heart of God, but we've missed His heart because we're so focused on being religious and pious. We've chosen rules and regulations, judgement and condemnation, over His grace. This is not dissimilar to how the crowd did when they said, "By law." Jesus has already fulfilled the law, so there's no reason for us to try to fulfill it ourselves, or try to "execute" those who we see are doing wrong. That's a wrong way of thinking.

Instead of us trying to carry out the law, let's live by His grace (Romans 6:14). Let's reveal who God really is—that even though we deserve death, He's given us life instead. That even though we deserve to be judged and stoned, to be condemned, He's given us another chance. We don't deserve His mercy, that woman didn't deserve it, but He gives it freely anyways. We need to let go of the stones we've been holding onto, so we can grasp who God truly is.

There is Now No Condemnation

There is therefore now no condemnation to those who are in Christ Jesus, who do not walk according to the flesh, but according to the Spirit. (Romans 8:1)

Condemnation now has no place in the life of the believer. This woman was condemned by law and we were condemned by unbelief

(John 3:17-18). It's what the crowd wanted and it's still what people want today. And yet we, as believers, no longer stand condemned. Why? Because the power of condemnation has been completely broken off of our lives. It has no place in our hearts.

Before we go on, we have to ask ourselves the definition of condemnation. Condemnation is defined by the Merriam-Webster's dictionary as "the expression of very strong disapproval, the act of condemning someone to punishment." You could also say it's saying that something or someone is not good enough. It is almost like rejection. But God says there is none of that for those who are in Christ. He's not going to condemn you. He's never going to look to punish you, or make you feel bad about yourself. You'll never be rejected by Him, and the only eyes He's going to look at you with are those filled with the same grace and compassion that Jesus showed to that woman. He's going to love you. He's going to forgive you. He's going to lift you back up.

Make no mistake. This doesn't mean God wants us to live in sinful lives, or commit crimes. God isn't going to excuse us from consequences. Notice how Jesus told the woman, "Go and sin no more." God doesn't give us grace for us to continue in sin, but to give us another chance, so we can get back up and do right with our lives.

44

It's time that we do the same. We need to extend grace to those who fall, and give them a chance to repent. Since there is no condemnation for those who are in Christ, and we are in Christ, no condemnation should come out of us. We shouldn't show that "strong and disapproving" look to anyone. We shouldn't say someone is not good enough. We shouldn't say they don't quite meet the standard.

Remember that at one point or another we were that person not doing right. How people live their lives does not give us grounds to condemn.

That doesn't mean we shouldn't correct (correction is an act of love after all) or simply accept sin, but it does mean that, should someone fall, grace should be given. Scripture says that "all have sinned and fall short of the glory of God" (Romans 3:23). That means us, too. So our job is not to condemn or judge. Our job is to love, to accept, and to receive, because that's what will draw people in. Scripture says it's the goodness of God that leads to repentance (Romans 2:4).

Condemnation, on the other hand, will do the opposite of what God wants—it will push people away, turn them off from Christ. It will hurt the people you hold dear. It'll reject the same people who we should be accepting. It's the opposite of who God is and it's time for it to end in our lives.

We need to love. We need to be open in our minds, and in our hearts for others. Not being open minded to sin, or that we approve of sin, but that we accept the people, just as they are, and let God do the changing. Remember, God hates sin, but He loves the people. Any change that happens won't be a result of you condemning someone, but from the freedom the love of God brings.

So the next time you see someone who is living in sin, let's follow the example of Jesus and love them first. Let's stop condemning people. People have experienced rejection and a disapproving look already in their lives. Let them feel accepted in Christ. That's what best represents the character, love, mercy, and grace of our God. No, we don't agree with their lifestyles, and yes, we will correct them in love according to scripture, but we need to let God's love draw people in. And we need to let Jesus do the judging.

Let Jesus Do the Judging

For the Father judges no one, but has committed all judgment to the

Son, (John 5:22)

Isn't it interesting that judgment has not been committed into the hands of man, but the hands of Jesus? Why do you think that is? I think it's because we don't have all the facts to make the necessary judgment. We don't judge like Jesus judges. Because His verdict is always grace. He alone has, had, and will continue to have the right to judge. He knows all the facts; He sees the things that no one else could see. Where others deal harshly, He will deal kindly and tenderly.

This doesn't mean He's oblivious to facts. It doesn't mean He doesn't know about the mistakes you've made. Jesus knows everything. He knew what the crowd wanted with that woman and knew the expected outcome. He heard the crowd, He heard the jeers, He saw the venom dripping from their lips, but nothing could change what His verdict would be. His verdict will always be grace. His sentence will always be mercy.

He's the most unfair judge in the world because He's always going to rule in your favor. If this world were a courtroom, He would be the defense and the judge. He's seen all the evidence, He's heard all the witnesses, but His focus is on something greater than all those things. He's looking at the blood He shed for you. The blood that's greater than any mistake, that's greater than any accusation. The case is rigged in your favor and the prosecution doesn't stand a chance because God is your defense. He's never lost a case, and your fate is in His hands—no better place for it to be.

All evidence is plain before Him. He sees the contents of your heart. He's all seeing, all hearing, and all understanding. And yet, sometimes, we act as though we are the divine judge. We act as though we have the right verdict and the right to condemn. We act like we have all the evidence and judgment has been committed into our hands. That we alone can make an accurate judgment based on the evidence presented.

The truth is—we don't. We can't see everything that's going on in hearts and minds like Jesus can. We can't see why people do what they do.

I love what one of the first pastors I was under, Pastor Kenny Foreman from Cathedral of Faith once said. I can't remember the exact quote, but he said something like this: "There are going to be three surprises when you get to heaven. One, that you made it. Two, people who you thought were going to be there, aren't. Three, the people who you thought weren't going to be there, are." The point of his statement? We don't have the ability to judge anyone, because although we may see the outer, we can't see the inner—their heart.

And because we can't see their heart, we say hurtful things out of ignorance. For example, when we see the homeless on the street we might say something like, "They should be out looking for a job." Or, "I can't believe they have their kids with them."

You don't know if living the streets is the best they can do for their family at that particular time in their life. Maybe the parents just lost their job, or they caught a bad break. You don't know if standing on that corner is all they can do. There's a reason that judgment has not been committed to you and me. We're unqualified to do so.

But we keep doing it, even though Matthew 7:1 says to "Judge not, that you be not judged." We inflict the pain of our judgment in God's name on people who need Jesus the most. We do so until they walk away from God, when God's desire is to draw people in just as they are. People stop seeing God as being loving and merciful, and instead see Him as angry, and ready to rain down holy judgment from above because of how we've represented Him. This isn't right. It does not portray who God really is.

Stop it. It's not your job to judge. It's your job to love. It's your job to demonstrate who Jesus is by extending the same grace and mercy that Christ showed that woman who was about to be stoned. Remember that at one time or another, we were that person not doing right, and yet God extended mercy to us. Remember that the same people that we've judged are the same people that Jesus laid His life on the cross for. He paid the price for their sin, our sin, when He didn't do anything wrong.

So drop the stones. Stop the condemnation and judgment. That's not who God is, and that can't be who we are. Judgment does not produce change. It'll never be condemnation that turns the hearts of man. It will always be His love, mercy, tenderness, and grace. The goodness of God leads people to repentance (Romans 2:4). We can't be beacons for judgment or condemnation anymore, and if we're persecuted, don't let it be because we're judgmental or mean, but because of righteousness (Matthew 5:10). Let's stop nitpicking flaws, and let God worry about fixing and repairing people. If we really want to show people where the answer is, let's point them to Jesus both in word, and how we live our lives.

Lift up those who fall. Love those who make mistakes. Stop the gossiping, the hurting, the pain, and follow the example that Jesus left for us. Remember, His love can never fail. His judgment is always grace. It's time we do the same.

Chapter 5: Right Where You Are

He'll Meet You There

Where can I go from Your Spirit? Or where can I flee from Your presence? If I ascend into heaven, You *are* there; If I make my bed in hell, behold, You *are there. If* I take the wings of the morning, *and* dwell in the uttermost parts of the sea, even there Your hand shall lead me, and Your right hand shall hold me. (Psalm 139:7-10)

Sometimes we think we've strayed too far away from God. We think we've reached just out of the extent of His hand. But that's not true. It's a lie from the pit of hell. There's no place you can go that's too far from God's love (Romans 8:38-39). You can't outreach His hand, you can't outreach His grace, and you can't outreach His mercy. There is nowhere you can go where He won't be with you.

Some of you may be on a path that looks dark. Some of you may be living in a personal hell right now. You may be feeling pain, or heartbreak. But how good is it to know, that God is still with you right in the midst of it? He won't leave you. He won't abandon you.

He won't forget about you.

He knows where you are in your life, right now, both mentally and spiritually. He understands your position better than you do. He knows why you are where you are, and He wants you to know that He's with you. Even when you can't feel Him, see Him, touch Him—He's there. He'll never leave you.

Even if others have shunned you, or closed the door on your face; God won't. Your mess won't scare God away. Your brokenness won't make Him cut and run. He's going to take care of you in your mess.

God doesn't ask that you clean up your mess by yourself. He's not expecting you to get it altogether by yourself. He wants to help.

Sometimes we think God has a "you spilled your milk, clean it up yourself" attitude. How messed up would our lives be if that were true? But that's not who God is. He's the God that will grab that mop and bucket and start cleaning it up for you, while at the same time bringing comfort and peace to your heart. Furthermore, He'll take the mistakes that you've made, and turn it into a blessing, into something that works to your good (Romans 8:28).

God is always going to meet you right where you are, so give your best right where you are. Your best might look different than mine. Your best might be saying, "God help me" when you can't seem to put down that drink. Or it might be, "God I need you" when you're in so much pain, that you don't know what to do. It doesn't matter what your situation. If you reach out to God right where you are, He's going to embrace you.

Think about this—Jesus went to the cross for you. Do you think there's a limit to what He'll do for you? There is no limit. There is no boundary that He won't cross. His goal isn't to punish you, but to help you, save you, and to deliver you. He's aggressively coming after you. His love is in constant pursuit of you. Through hell, high water, pain, or suffering, be ready. Because when you call, He'll come for you.

He's Looking at Your Heart

But the LORD said to Samuel, "Do not look at his appearance or at the height of his stature, because I have refused him. For *the Lord does* not *see* as man sees; for man looks at the outward appearance, but the LORD looks at the heart." (1 Samuel 16:7)

Some of us may feel a sense of shame with what we have to offer to God. We see other people lifting their hands to heaven, speaking in tongues and doing everything right. They look so perfect. However, it doesn't matter what you might see on the outside. The outside is not relevant to God.

It doesn't matter to God how high your hands may be raised, how loud you clap, or how high you jump. God's not looking at any of that. He looks at your heart.

So then we begin to ask ourselves, "What is God asking for? If He doesn't want me jumping up and down for Him, then what is He really looking for? What does He want?" God wants your heart. If God has your heart, He has everything.

You see, you could be jumping up and down, dancing and doing all this stuff before the Lord, but if what's inside isn't matching what's on the outside, all you're doing is wasting energy. You don't have to fake it for God. Remove that pressure of being fake before God. All God wants is for you to be real. Give Him what you have— no matter how small it may seem to you. If your heart is in it—it's a huge thing to Him.

God understands if your best looks different at the various stages in your life. No matter where you may be, just seek Him with everything that you have, give Him everything you have. And don't compare your best to someone else's. It's wrong to do so. No two people's lives are exactly the same. We all go through things at different times and speeds. Everyone is valuable to God right where they are.

Let's look at an example of this.

Now Jesus sat opposite the treasury and saw how the people put money into the treasury. And many *who were* rich put in much. Then one poor widow came and threw in two mites, which make a quadrans. So He called His disciples to *Himself* and said to them, "Assuredly, I say to you that this poor widow has put in more than all those who have given to the treasury; for they all put in out of their abundance, but she out of her poverty put in all that she had, her whole livelihood." (Mark 12:41-44)

Wouldn't it be unreasonable for Jesus to ask this woman in the scripture to give as much as everyone else? That's not what Jesus was looking for. What He was looking for was for someone to give from all of their heart. Jesus saw that this woman had, and God acknowledged her sacrifice. He knew she wasn't holding anything back, but that she was giving everything, from her place of poverty.

That's how God is with us. Some of us are in that place of poverty—we don't have much to offer God. It may look puny in comparison to someone else's gifts, but it's still everything that we have. It doesn't matter what it looks like in the natural. Even if what you're giving might look like pennies, if God sees that you're giving everything—He sees riches.

Notice God didn't say that those putting in the most money were the ones who gave the most. The one who gave the most was the one who appeared to give the least. He saw the purity of this woman's heart.

That's the kind of God we serve. The God who is merciful, and also understanding. Where others fail to understand, how good is it to know that God's understanding does not? God understands everything because He's the only one that can truly see your heart. Don't be ashamed of what you have to give to God. It doesn't matter if it looks small and insignificant to you, or to others, because it's significant to God.

From The Inside Out

Also He spoke this parable to some who trusted in themselves that they were righteous, and despised others: "Two men went up to the temple to pray, one a Pharisee and the other a tax collector. The Pharisee stood and prayed thus with himself, 'God, I thank You that I am not like other men--extortioners, unjust, adulterers, or even as this tax collector. I fast twice a week; I give tithes of all that I possess.' And the tax collector, standing afar off, would not so much as raise *his* eyes to heaven, but beat his breast, saying, 'God, be merciful to me a sinner!' I tell you, this man went down to his house justified *rather* than the other; for everyone who exalts himself will be humbled, and he who humbles himself will be exalted." (Luke 18:9-14)

Blind Pharisee, first cleanse the inside of the cup and dish, that the outside of them may be clean also. (Matthew 23:26)

We make every effort to make sure our outside looks good. That every spot is clean, and that we're all nice and polished. We don't say certain words and we don't do certain things. It's almost as if we're afraid. Afraid of being who we really are before God. Remember the verse about all falling short of the glory of God (Romans 3:23)? So why do we try to hide our mess from God? Why do we try to shine ourselves up for Him? That isn't what God wants.

According to Scripture, God wants you to be open and messed up right where you are before Him. He wants to meet you where you truly are in your heart so He can produce a genuine change inside of your life.

It's okay to be open with God like the tax collector. It's okay to say, "God I have a problem with my tongue. I swear like a sailor." Or perhaps, "God, I have a problem with alcohol, but here I am God, I want to change. Change me, Lord. Help me."

We don't need to hide who we are anymore from God. We don't have to act clean on the outside before Him. You can't surprise Him, and He already sees what you may be trying to hide from Him. After all, He made us. Do you really think you can hide from Him? Instead of focusing so hard on being who you are not, let Him see the real you so He can work on you—so you can be at your best for Him.

But if you don't acknowledge your problem before God, how can we expect to receive the help we need? You'll be just like the Pharisees. If you ignore the problems, the dirt of your heart will never come clean. God wants you to be open about where your heart is, not to shame you, but so He can meet you right there.

You see, change isn't something that starts from the outside in. It's something that occurs from the inside out—when God starts changing your heart. When He works on you from the inside out, the outer will come into alignment.

People will see something genuine begin to shift, to change inside of your life. They'll see that the same person they loved going to the bar with now no longer desires the drink. They'll see the person who used to chase after women, begin to chase after God. They'll see the impossible things that only God can do take place in your life.

But God can't clean you if you claim that you're already clean. You have to see the problem for yourself, acknowledge it before Him, and let Him take care of it. We don't have to pretend anymore. We don't have to act like everything is perfect or that we have it altogether. We don't have to dress impeccably on the outside so no one can see the brokenness on the inside. We can be real. We can let

God meet us where we are, and clean us up like no one else can. He can and will do something real in your live—something genuine—if you let Him. Aren't you tired of living behind a façade?

It's time to drop the act and be open before God. Stop focusing so much on the outside. Stop trying to be the "good Christian", and focus on what's going on inside your heart. Stop living to project to others that you're "good" and start living for God.

Don't be afraid of what you see. It may not look pretty at the moment, but just wait till God gets His hands on you. You're going to be clean. You're going to be pure. You're going to be changed.

Don't be scared that you're too messy or dirty to be cleaned up. God saw all that gunk, all that mess, all that dirt, before He sent His Son to die for you, and He still saw that you were worth it. Even if He had to make that decision all over again, He'd do it again for you. There's nothing that can make Him stop loving you. You can be openly dirty before Him. It's not going to make Him love you any less.

God wants you to come to Him right where you are, so He can meet you right where you're really at—dirt, grime and all. He wants to change you, from the inside out. Will you come before Him, and let Him?

Come as You Are

"Ho! Everyone who thirsts, Come to the waters; and you who have no money, Come, buy and eat. Yes, come, buy wine and milk without money and without price. (Isaiah 55:1)

The problem is not that God is distant from us. The problem is that we haven't come to Him. He's done His part. It isn't that He doesn't have the door open for you. He's not cold and distant. He's definitely not running away from you. The problem is us. We would rather run from Him than come to Him.

Sometimes it's because we're afraid. We've done so much wrong in our lives we feel there is no way the door can be open to us. Sometimes we think we've closed the door ourselves. Or we've dropped the ball too many times. We feel like there is no way we could present ourselves before God. We're just too messed up to do so.

But that's not true. Our mistakes, and our failures, are not enough to "separate us from the love of God which is in Christ Jesus our Lord" (Romans 8:38-39). The punishment that was supposed to be on you, on me, went on Jesus at the cross of Calvary instead. The price has been paid. Sin has been defeated. You can no longer use the excuse that you stay away from God because of your sins and failures because that has been taken away. The path is clear for you to come home to God.

Whether you know God or not, the door is open. If you feel God drawing your heart, like His Word says only He can (John 6:44), don't hesitate. Just come. Come to the waters and be satisfied. Don't look for something to fill the hole that only God can fulfill. Don't disqualify yourself. Your mistakes are of little importance to God. When He looks at you, He doesn't see your mistakes. He sees a masterpiece. He sees you. He sees someone with purpose, and someone with a destiny. He sees someone too precious to live a lifetime without, and His desire is that you come to Him.

You don't have to wait to hear a thundering voice. Time and place doesn't matter. He just wants you. Not just for a day, not just for a couple months or even years, but forever.

But God is so good that He'll never force Himself on you.

God won't violate your free will. Some of us have that mentality of being forced into church, or forced to do "Christian things." Yes, you should raise up your kids in the way you should go, but there comes a point in life when people have to choose God for themselves. God wants people to come from a place of freedom, not of obligation.

Why? Because just like how God didn't force Adam to not eat the forbidden fruit, He's not going to force you to come to Him. He may tug at your heart, but even as He tugs, the choice is still in your hands. This is a choice you have to make for yourself.

What will you choose today? Are you going to take a leap? The door is open. Jesus has opened the door for all humanity to have the opportunity to come to God.

Stop hiding and come as you are.

The invitation is open. You are welcomed and accepted. You have a home inside of Him.

Chapter 6: He Loves You Too Much To Leave You There

He's Shaping You Towards Your Destiny

The word which came to Jeremiah from the LORD, saying: "Arise and go down to the potter's house, and there I will cause you to hear My words." Then I went down to the potter's house, and there he was, making something at the wheel. And the vessel that he made of clay was marred in the hand of the potter; so he made it again into another vessel, as it seemed good to the potter to make. Then the word of the LORD came to me, saying: "O house of Israel, can I not do with you as this potter?" says the LORD. "Look, as the clay *is* in the potter's hand, so *are* you in My hand, O house of Israel! (Jeremiah 18:1-6)

For we are His workmanship, created in Christ Jesus for good works, which God prepared beforehand that we should walk in them. (Ephesians 2:10)

God loves you right where you are, but we need to remember that God loves you too much to leave you there. You are the clay in the palm of His hands and are constantly being molded and shaped for His purposes. You are continuously in a process of refinement and fire, too. The fire is not meant to burn you, but to purify and break off things that are holding you back.

Why is God doing this? He is shaping you towards your divine destiny inside of Him. In order to get where God is taking you, He needs to remove the things that are holding you back, the things that are not like Him. The bumps and bruises you receive on this walk of life are shaping and guiding you to where you need to be. It might not always be pretty, you might not see where your life is going, or why you are where you are, but God wants you to know you're still in His hands. There's purpose. It's all part of His process.

However, in the midst of the process you might ask yourself why there is so much hurt and pain. Pain is not necessarily a result of you doing something wrong. Pain can also be the result of God setting things in your life in the right way. Just like how a patient feels pain when a doctor resets a broken bone, we will feel pain when God is setting our life into the path He always intended for us.

Don't get me wrong. Sometimes we're in pain because of choices that we've made in our lives. God has given us free will after all. But what I'm saying, is that when you're in the potter's hands, when you're in the hand of the gardener who's pruning you (John 15:2), you may feel pain, you may be uncomfortable. Why? Because God has to take us outside of our comfort zone in order to promote growth. It's all part of the process.

Look at David. Do you think he didn't feel pain when his own father-in-law, who he had faithfully been serving under, tried to kill him with a spear? But David had to be separated from King Saul. He had to go through the things he went through in the wilderness to get to the point where God could make him king.

He's shaping you to reach your full potential inside of Him. He doesn't want to let you live your life as a twig—not accomplishing your purpose. He wants you to fulfill the plan and purpose He has for your life, to grow into a mighty oak tree that towers to the skies. But you'll never get there by staying in the same place. You must be changed. You must be shaped. You must be prepared for where God wants to take you.

You probably will suffer. Jesus said that "in this world you shall have tribulation" (John 16:33), and scripture also states that "many are the afflictions of the righteous" (Psalm 34:19). But God also says to be of good cheer, because He has overcome the world (John 16:33), and that He will deliver us in those very same scriptures.

So trust His hand. Trust that He's cutting the branches in your life that don't need to be there. Trust that He's shaping you with vision in mind. Believe that any fire you're going through, is simply to purify you. Trust in His sovereignty.

God is Sovereign

Are not two sparrows sold for a copper coin? And not one of them falls to the ground apart from your Father's will. But the very hairs of your head are all numbered. Do not fear therefore; you are of more value than many sparrows. (Matthew 10:29-31)

God is sovereign. Provided you have God as Lord over your life, and you've given control to Him, your life is under His rule. It's no longer under your command. What God has allowed to happen in your life, has purpose behind it. And even the mistakes that you have made in your life, God can turn around and use for something to His glory. God is King over all.

Look at what the scripture says. God is watching over two little birds, and not one of them falls without God allowing it. God says you carry more value than many sparrows. Think about how much He thinks about you. You are of great worth to Him. You are valuable. Whatever God has allowed to take place in your life is not a mistake. He doesn't look at your situation and say "Oops." Even when you choose to exhibit your free will, He can still utilize that for His purpose.

You might look at your situation and say, "I don't see how this can work to my good. How can God use this pain, this tragedy, to my advantage? God looks like an unfair God." Although it may not look like it at that time, since God allowed it to happen—even free will choices—He's going to use it for your good (Romans 8:28). The real test of trusting the sovereignty of God comes when we are at our lowest point. Will we believe when everything seems to be going wrong?

You see, it's easy to say, "God is sovereign" when everything is going okay, but it's harder to say the same when things look disastrous. Can we truly say that God is in control of everything when a child dies, when friends walk away, or when we have to make painful decisions? Can you, with all your heart, say, "God knew this would happen," or "God can make something good come from this" when it happens to you?

In the midst of the bad things that happen in life, it's important to remember that nothing will ever change that fact that God is on the throne. God does not forget to intervene. He's still sovereign, and God can use where you are for His purpose.

Let's go further into King David's story. He was anointed by the prophet Samuel when he was a boy to be king over all of Israel. I'm sure David might have been thinking, "This is where my life takes off. Things are going to be smooth sailing from here on out."

Now think of his reaction when the opposite came true. Once he was anointed, opposition like never before began to rise up against him. It started off with a giant. A problem that was greater than anything he had faced before. Then after victory over the impossible, King Saul, now his father-in-law, tried to kill him and drove him away from his home and wife. David proceeded to live among the enemies he had slain in the Philistines. He was in a constant state of danger for almost fifteen years! He could have thought at any given time, "How did I get to where I am? Where is that promise? God, if You're still on the throne, why is all this stuff happening to me? I never asked for this."

David couldn't see it at the time, but God, in His sovereignty, allowed all those things to happen because they were shaping David for his destiny. He received the promise as a boy at about fifteen years old, but it came to fulfillment when he was a man of thirty. God matured David, to take him where God promised he would go. God allowed all these things to happen because God had great things in store for David.

The same goes for you. The reason God, in all His sovereignty, is allowing you to go through times in the wilderness, to go through painful times, is because it's what is needed to get you where you need to be.

You see, the process to get to your destiny isn't a straight path from point A to point B. It's a path filled with mountain highs, and valley lows. It may look sometimes as though you've made a wrong turn, and that there's no way God wants you to be where you are. But if God is guiding your steps, and put you where you are (rather than your own poor decisions), God has a reason for it. And even if your own poor decisions got you where you are, God can still get you on the right track. Not only that, He can use what you went through, for your good.

The path God has you on is not always an easy path. But remember, God, in His sovereignty, has allowed you to be there. Your steps have been ordered.

Your Steps Are Ordered

The steps of a *good* man are ordered by the LORD, And He delights in his way. (Psalm 37:23)

Your steps have been ordered by God, even when it doesn't look like they have. Let's go back to David and think about how God ordered His steps. We'll see how God used the things that looked bad, and turned them into something good.

When Saul threw a spear at David, it essentially separated David from King Saul. This separation allowed David to start his path to becoming king. In his journey in the wilderness, he discovered his army, which would be come to known as his mighty men. In the same travels, he found one of his wives, Abigail, to replace the one that he had lost. Things that originally seemed bad—running away from his home, being chased—were turned into something good for David. What he went through prepared him for the promise that God had provided. David gained more than he lost as he continued on the path that was ordered of God. There was purpose for every battle and step that David took. He grew and matured on the journey. It was a journey that no one but God could have orchestrated, and God will do the same for you.

Remember there is a plan for your life and God fully intends on making it come to pass. But there's going to be mess, heartbreak and hurt. You're going to get those bumps and bruises, but God has promised to be with you every step of the way.

He has guided you to where you are now, and He's still guiding the steps you are going to take in the future. Trust Him, there is a purpose behind why you are where you are. The suffering you may be feeling right now, is a direct correlation to how far and high you're going in the future.

Sometimes we get comfortable walking about in the same steps, stagnating in our Christian walk. We go to church every Sunday, but we aren't advancing, we aren't achieving the purposes and dreams that God has placed in our lives. You might be telling yourself, "I've lived my life like this for as long as I can remember." God has no intention of letting you live the same way all your life. He wants you to always be advancing, to go where you've never gone before. But in order to get you where you've never been before, you have to go through things you've never gone through before. God has no intention of letting you walk in circles. He wants to get you to the fulfillment of the promises in your heart that He put there, to get you to your destination. Your journey may take you through strange and foreign lands, as it did David, but, rest assured, that even in the unfamiliar, God is ordering your steps. He's still with you.

This is further demonstrated in the Israelites journey to the promised land. They were on a route they had never been on before. All they saw was wilderness. They had no guide points of where they were going, nor did they have a map. This was uncharted ground, and yet it didn't change the fact that God had ordered their steps to be there, and that He was ordering their steps while they were there. God was that pillar of cloud that guided them by day, and that pillar of fire by night. God was consistent in always guiding each of their steps. But God didn't just take them through the wilderness to get to the promised land. God took them into the wilderness with purpose.

The reason a thirteen-day journey took forty years for the Israelites was because that was how long it took for them to change. God did not want their old, set-in ways to transfer into the promised land. There were things among the Israelites that had to die out, before they could walk into the promise. They couldn't go into the promised land being the same unbelieving, cow worshipping people they were before. The wilderness had to first be taken out of them before they got to what God had promised.

What does this mean for us? It means we will go through times of wilderness, too, before we can get to the promised land of our lives. Sometimes God orders our steps where we don't want to go. He does this so that things that are not like Him will die out from our lives. Each one of us has those kind of things in our lives. For some, it may be fear, or it may be cheating, or lying. It's as varied as every person, but one thing remains the same: God will guide you into the wilderness, until that thing that is not like Him dies and you change. It's not going to be easy, but it's necessary. Times of fire and difficulty, burn off those things that aren't like Him.

Fire Sets You Free

And these three men, Shadrach, Meshach, and Abed-Nego, fell down bound into the midst of the burning fiery furnace. Then King Nebuchadnezzar was astonished; and he rose in haste *and* spoke, saying to his counselors, "Did we not cast three men bound into the midst of the fire?" They answered and said to the king, "True, O king." "Look!" he answered, "I see four men loose, walking in the midst of the fire; and they are not hurt, and the form of the fourth is like the Son of God." (Daniel 3:23-25)

We ask ourselves why we have to go through fire, or times of extreme difficulty. We suffer through times where we feel we're being pushed to our absolute limit, times where the only thing that's kept us alive and sane is the grace of God. What's the purpose? Why do we go through things that seem like they are going to kill us?

The purpose is clear according to scripture.

Fire means you're going to experience a new period and season of freedom, of promotion. It's a place of transition, an in-between from where you are now to where God is trying to move you. Before these three men were thrown into the fire, they were bound, but once they emerged from the fire, they were free.

You see, times of fire aren't designed to hurt you, but to set you free from whatever has been binding or stopping you from achieving what God wants you to achieve, to get you to a higher place. It may not be comfortable, and it's probably not something you'll want to go through, but it's necessary to get where God wants to take you.

Once again, it's all part of the process.

Let's use the process of purifying gold to demonstrate. Gold is purified by going through fire. As gold is in the fire, the impurities begin to come to the top so they can be removed. The gold becomes purer because of it. However, when gold doesn't go through the fire, those impurities remain. It doesn't look as beautiful as it could. It hasn't reached its full potential. But fire helps it get there. Fire is necessary to get the gold in its purest state.

Now let's apply that to us. You are that gold. When you go through the fire—hard times, grief, losses—things in your life that are impure, such as bad mindsets, habits, or false beliefs rise to the top so God can remove them. You begin to look more and more like Christ, because all the things that are not like God, all the impurities, are being dealt with.

Once the season of refinement has passed, you can move forward into the promises of God. The fire is to your benefit. It's not to burn you, or to kill you, but to set you free, to purify you. God doesn't put you through the fire because He's a mean God, but because He's a loving God. He loves you too much to leave you where you are with things that hold you back or hinder you. He wants you to experience the good things He has for you on the other side.

Just look at what was on the other side of that fire for Shadrach, Meshach, and Abednego. The same king that was going to kill them, God used to promote them. Not only that, God was glorified when the king admits that "there is no other God who can deliver like this," and that "any people, nation, or language which speaks anything amiss against the God of Shadrach, Meshach, and Abed-Nego shall be cut in pieces, and their houses shall be made an ash heap" (Daniel 3:29). These men were taken to a higher place, exalted, experiencing God's best for their lives. But these three men would have missed out on it if they had never experienced the fire.

Just remember as you go through the fire, that God allowed you to go through what you're going through because He loves you. He's refining you for a purpose, for your destiny, and your future. He loves you too much to simply let you struggle in the hurt and despair, the fire, without making a new product at the end.

I know it may not be comforting when we think that God allows us to go through fire in our lives. However, what's comforting is the fact that He's going to be with you in the fire.

Did you notice that the king saw *four* men within the fire? The three men who were thrown into the furnace, and a fourth man walking amongst them, (Daniel 3:25), who is "like the Son of God." They were not alone! You are not alone. He's closer to you than ever during those times of purification. He is walking alongside you. He will not abandon you.

You may not see the benefits of the fire while you're going through it. You might be feeling things you don't want to feel and it may seem like a living hell, but trust and believe that God is using it to purify you. He's using it to release you into your destiny. It's working for your good.

All Things Work to Your Good

And we know that all things work together for good to those who love God, to those who are the called according to *His* purpose. (Romans 8:28)

As you go through your times of fire, or endure the bumps on the road, it's important to remember that because you love God, and have been called according to His purpose, all things are working toward your good.

I love how scripture says "all things." Including, and, often times, the bad things. Bad things will still happen to God's people, but God promises that it will all still work on your behalf. You may be going through something painful, something that at times doesn't even make sense to you, but God will still use it for your good. God can turn everything—every single thing—into something good for you.

Let's look at this demonstrated in the life of Joseph. Joseph was betrayed by his brothers, sold as a slave, accused of sleeping with his master's wife, and was thrown in jail for a crime he didn't commit (Genesis 37-40). Yet God used those same exact things to position him for what God would do in his life.

All of Joseph's previous experiences, shaped and matured Joseph so he would be in position to receive what God had promised. Joseph being tossed in jail, put him in a position to interpret Pharaoh's dream. Because he was able to interpret Pharaoh's dream, he was exalted to being second in command in Egypt. What once seemed like a hopeless situation—jail—had been used by God to further Joseph's place in working for God's purposes. And it was all working for his good.

Joseph couldn't see that at the time, but the guidance and the hand of God never stopped being on Joseph's life. Everything Joseph went through was necessary for God's purpose.

The same applies to you. Some of you may be feeling like so many bad things have been happening to you. It just seems to be bad break after bad break. Just when you think things are getting better, something happens and they get worse. Let me tell you this: the hand of God is still on your life. He's not leaving you during these tough times you're going through. What you're going through is necessary, so God can bring fulfillment to what He has promised to you. What you're going through is just positioning you.

So keep your faith in Him, keep your belief in the Lord. You are where you are on purpose, and He wants to take you to where you've never been before.

Chapter 7: God Can Use You

You Are Qualified

Who shall bring a charge against God's elect? *It is* God who justifies. (Romans 8:33)

Not that we are sufficient of ourselves to think of anything as *being* from ourselves, but our sufficiency *is* from God, (2 Corinthians 3:5)

Sometimes we look at our past, our mistakes, and we say to ourselves, "There is no way God can use me." We disqualify ourselves. We say that we aren't good enough. We are unqualified. We sometimes even bring charges against ourselves. We give reasons why we can't do this or why we can't do that. We think that we cannot be used by God because of our past mistakes. We are unqualified, or are unjustified. We are our own worst enemy.

The truth is that, yes, we are all horribly unqualified. On our own, we are not fit to serve the Lord. But glory to God, our qualifications are not based on what we do, what other people say, on our

85

accomplishments, or on our failures—it's based on Him.

Your justification comes from Almighty God. Since there is nothing greater than God, nothing is great enough to disqualify you. You are justified. You *are* qualified in Christ. You are enabled to do His will because of God alone (Romans 8:30).

We need to shed off the mindset that we cannot be of use to God. Let me tell you this. It doesn't matter what you've done, or not done, said, or not said—God still has a plan for you. He still wants to do great things in your life. He knows about your past. He knows about your mistakes. But those things don't matter to Him. He wants to use you and He has a calling for your life. The reason you're able to answer and fulfill the call isn't because you're a good person, but because God has called you.

You might be saying, "I've seen what no one else has. I know me. I can't do it." Let me respond by saying that when God calls you, He has already considered every part of who you are. Some of you disqualify yourselves because of all the things you know about yourself.

God has already seen all those things you're so worried about. He sees your innermost thoughts and feelings—good and bad. But those things don't matter to Him. If God can use a prostitute like Rahab, an adulterer like David, a murderer like Moses...He can use you. He's seen all the things in your life that aren't right and loves you anyway. God isn't looking at your mess; He's looking at your future. God has seen the end, from the beginning. You are qualified. You are justified. God can use you.

You Are the Righteousness of God

For He made Him who knew no sin *to be* sin for us, that we might become the righteousness of God in Him. (2 Corinthians 5:21)

Some of us don't believe we can be used by God because we're unrighteous. We say or do things that are wrong. Maybe we slip and fall. But scripture says that you are the righteousness of God in Christ Jesus. When God sent His Son to die for you, He put you in right standing with Him. Your righteousness is not based on you; it's based on the unshakable cross. Nothing can change that.

How amazing is it that God used the Perfect One, the one who knew no sin, to get us in right standing with Him? Consider that uneven exchange. Look at how backward the Kingdom of God is by our standards. The Kingdom of God is not based on anything you and I do. It's based on what Jesus did on the cross.

That's why it's impossible to say you're not the righteousness of God, because you are not the standard. Jesus is. When you believe in Jesus and all He has done for you, you become the righteousness of God. This doesn't mean you're going to be perfect, and it doesn't mean you won't fall or make mistakes. What it means is that even if you do make a mistake, it cannot change what God has spoken. You see, our justification isn't based on our own righteousness. According to scripture, our righteousness, is comparable to filthy rags (Isaiah 64:6). God does not want us to be dependent on ourselves, on our own holiness and righteousness. He wants us to focus on the cross and its implications for our lives. It's not about getting, it's all about receiving. Jesus' death on the cross is a gift that has been given to you.

This doesn't mean that you'll feel like you're the righteousness of God every day. Some days you'll feel like the worst sinner in the world. But, praise God, this righteousness is not based on something as unstable as feelings. It's not determined by your flesh and soul.

It's not determined by your past, or by your mistakes. It's determined by Jesus and what He did for you. So don't say you can't do it because you've made too many mistakes. Don't say you can't do it because you've messed up one too many times. God doesn't see those mistakes. He sees His Son. And sees you as the righteousness of God.

God Uses the Weak to Shame the Strong

But God has chosen the foolish things of the world to put to shame the wise, and God has chosen the weak things of the world to put to shame the things which are mighty; and the base things of the world and the things which are despised God has chosen, and the things which are not, to bring to nothing the things that are, that no flesh should glory in His presence. (1 Corinthians 1:27-29)

Now that we've gotten rid of the excuse of not being "righteous enough" to be used by God, let's deal with another excuse. Some of you look at yourselves and see that there's no way God can use you because you're weak. All your life you've been told that you're insignificant. You've been rejected, made fun of, and picked last. How could anyone use someone like you? I have great news. God loves to use people *just like you.*

God doesn't care if you're the smallest of the small. He doesn't care if everyone else has rejected you. He doesn't care how unqualified you may be. God still wants to use you for His glory.

God uses the runts, the rejects, and the weak to shame those who are strong. Flesh can't get the glory for something that only God can do. God shows His strength the most when He uses the least. That's why scripture says, "No flesh should glory in His presence" (1 Corinthians 1:29). The extraordinary doesn't happen because of the might of man, but because of the might of God.

We see how God uses the small to do great things once again in the story of King David and his army. We remember their great feats, the great things they accomplished, but they didn't start off that way. In their beginning, in their origin, they were all broken people.

And everyone *who was* in distress, everyone who *was* in

debt, and everyone *who was* discontented gathered to him. So he became captain over them. And there were about four hundred men with him. (1 Samuel 22:2)

Unlike other kings, who inherited armies when they took the throne, David met his army in an unusual place—a cave. They weren't mighty warriors, they were broken just like you and me. They were messed up. They had problems. But what was important wasn't their problems and issues, but who they gathered themselves around. They gathered around someone who was like Christ, and because of that, they became mighty as a result. They did things that were superhuman. Things that hadn't been done before. All thanks to Christ.

Let's apply that to ourselves. Some of you are just like these future mighty men. Some of you are in debt, hurting, angry, broken, or messed up. But just because you're messed up doesn't mean God can't use you. It doesn't mean your purpose and destiny has been diminished. On the contrary, these men's brokenness and pain led them into their purpose and destiny.

What do I mean? If they were not in the state in which they were, who knows if they would have aligned themselves with David. And if they hadn't lined up with David, God's own man, they would have missed out on what God had in store for them. Brokenness is not a curse. Pain is not a curse. These heartaches can lead us right to where God wants us to be.

Turns out their brokenness was only temporary. There was a turnaround in their situation. They became David's elite force. Many of them went on to become David's mighty men, whole and complete. Champions who accomplished the impossible, who did what was previously unheard of.

Some of you may be in a period of brokenness and pain and it doesn't seem like it's going to end. Let me encourage you—that pain, that hurt, is just temporary. It's not going to last forever. It's leading you right to where God wants you to be—to Him. That pain is going to work for your good if you trust in the Lord, and keep yourself close to Him.

You might be feeling weak right now, but that's perfect. God uses the weak, people like you, to shame the strong. God doesn't use those who look great through their own strength. He uses the people from whom He'll get the most glory. He uses those who appear to be nothing. He chooses you.

You Were Created For a Purpose

"Before I formed you in the womb I knew you; before you were born I sanctified you; I ordained you a prophet to the nations." (Jeremiah 1:5)

Did you know that God assigned you to a purpose before you were even put in your mother's womb? Your life is not a mistake. You are not an accident. God already had a purpose and plan for your life before your parents even met.

Don't believe that we are merely existing, or that we'll depart without leaving a mark on the world. There are certain jobs that only you are qualified to do. There are certain things that God has designed expressly for you.

God wants to shape and mold you for His purpose. You might not always look pretty during the process, but do we think that God is shaping us just for show? Or that God is making a vessel simply for decoration? That's not how God works. God doesn't make anything without a purpose. You are crafted for where God wants to take you.

So don't sit there wishing that God would use you how He used someone else. No two vessels are going to be exactly the same, but that doesn't mean any vessel is less valuable than the other. You might use a spoon more than a can opener, but that doesn't make it any less valuable or less useful. Sometimes a spoon is the better tool, sometimes it's the can opener—it depends on the job. And there are some jobs that can only be done by you. You're being crafted, towards a greater purpose than you could ever imagine.

For we are His workmanship, created in Christ Jesus for good works, which God prepared beforehand that we should walk in them. (Ephesians 2:10)

Keep in mind, that when God made you, He had a complete purpose in mind. That means, all the little quips, all your mannerisms, all the intrinsic details that make you who you are, are provided for a purpose. He shaped and is shaping you the way He did for a reason.

In light of that, we need to learn to love who God made us to be. Don't despise yourself because you aren't a preacher. Don't look down on yourself because you aren't gifted in singing. Not everyone is assigned to be a preacher or work in ministry. God made some of His children to be businessmen, scientists, scholars…all these jobs can be used to fulfill God's purposes here on earth, and bring glory to God. Stay in the lane where God designed for you to be. And love who God made.

I love how the scripture says that God has prepared your steps before you walk in them. In other words, He's seen all the steps you will ever take, and no matter how off course it may seem you are, because your steps have been ordered by Him, there's a purpose to be fulfilled at the end.

In addition to that, He also sees all the missteps you will make along the way. He sees every time you will fall flat on your face. But as long as your heart, and your life, is set on Him, there will still be fulfillment to the purpose that He made for you.

You might not understand how it's going to be fulfilled, but you just have to trust that God is going to get you to the fulfillment. He wants to use you, but the shaping process isn't always a straight line. At times it may look like the opposite of the promise is happening.

But trust that even when you run into times like that, you're there on purpose. God wants to use you. What you're going through is shaping you so He can use you for His glory. Don't let worry sidetrack you. Let God be your guide. Let God use you. Let God be in control. You aren't unqualified. You aren't too weak to be used. You're perfect, for what He has in store for you.

Chapter 8: God Is Your Helper

He's Going to Come Through

For I, the LORD your God, will hold your right hand, saying to you, 'Fear not, I will help you.' (Isaiah 41:13)

It's easy to think that God has left you alone in the midst of your trouble. There's just so much pain, and you don't know where God could be at a time like this. Why hasn't He come through yet? Doesn't He see what you're going through? Doesn't He care about what you are facing? Is He going to help you or not?

At those times, when it seems as though God has abandoned you, He's actually closer to you than the air you breathe. He will never leave you. He's holding your hand. He's with you right now, giving you grace for the day, peace for your torment, and love for your fears.

During our struggles, we need to remember that God will always come through for you. Your problem, your situation, is not greater than His promise. It might seem like there is no solution to what you're going through, that what you're going through is never going to end, but let me tell you this: God is the solution, when the problem seems impossible.

There will be times in our lives when we will encounter these God-sized problems. We're going to run into things that only God can fully and truly understand. When we run into these problems, it's important to remember that if God brought you to it, He's going to bring you all the way through it.

Even if you can't even begin to understand what you're going through, or why you're going through it, remember that He understands. He's going to take care of your problem for His utmost glory. He's going to cross every "T," and dot every single "I." When God takes care of something, He takes care of it to the very last detail.

Let's remember David and Goliath. Before David slayed Goliath, Goliath looked like problem that would never be remedied. He towered over the people of God, tormenting them for forty days. I'm sure the Israelites were thinking, "Where are You God? Where are You when we're facing someone who's greater than anything we've faced before? I thought You said You would come through for us. We thought we were You're chosen people, but where are You now?"

What they didn't know was that God had already prepared David for Goliath, fifteen years in advance. In other words, God already had the answer, before the problem even occurred.

Let's apply that to ourselves. Your problem already has a solution. It doesn't matter how big or strong it might look to you. It doesn't matter how gigantic it may seem. When you trust in God, you'll see that God is greater than anything, and He can do what no one else can do. You're going to see Him come through for you.

You'll see that He is faithful, He's reliable, that He heard your cry when that enemy was tormenting you, taunting you. You'll see that He knew what you were going through, how much pain you were in, and that He was going to save you.

You know what else you'll see? That giant that you thought would never come down? You will see defeated, with its head cut off before your very eyes. You'll enjoy the victory on the other side of that giant. What a God we serve.

God is fighting your battles for you right now, and because God is fighting your battles, the victory has already been won. Your victory is at hand. God is your helper. He is your answer, and He's holding your hand in the midst of your trial.

He Will Hold Your Hand

"For I, the LORD your God, will hold your right hand..." (Isaiah 41:13)

Some of you may feel that you are all alone in what you're going through, and that no one could possibly understand your situation. Victory seems unattainable. It feels like God is absent from your life. But God wants you to know that the opposite is true. He understands what you're going through and wants you to know that you aren't alone. He's going to get you through to the other side of your situation. His fingers are interlocked with your own. He's never left you. He wants you to know that everything is going to be okay.

Perhaps one of the worst things to feel as you're going through hard times is the feeling of being alone. It's easy to think that way and many of us do. Thank God Almighty that, according to scripture, we are never alone. God is with us *always,* especially during the most trying times in our lives. This doesn't mean your life will be easy, or that things will be fair, but God will be with you in every step. Even when you don't have the strength to hold onto Him, He's going to hold onto you.

God wants you to know that you have never been alone. Even during the times when you felt like you were alone, when you asked, "God where are you?" He was there. When you were struggling, in pain, asking yourself, "If God is really there, then why hasn't He done anything? Why hasn't He helped me? Why has He let all this happen to me? Where was He when I needed Him most?" He was there. Just because you didn't feel Him, doesn't mean He wasn't there, or He wasn't listening. Think about a time when you were at your lowest point. Did someone help you, encourage you, or give you a hand? That was God helping. He heard your prayers.

And believe me, when you keep your trust and belief in God, there will be a time where you won't just see the comfort of His hand, and the encouragement it brings, but you'll also feel the strength of it. You'll see deliverance in your life from what has been challenging you for so long. You'll see the David defeat your Goliath. You'll see the impossible come to pass in your life. You'll see the God who is mighty to save, the God of miracles.

So don't give up. He's still helping you. He's still holding your hand. Everything is going to be okay. Don't be discouraged when you go through pain. And when you feel alone, consider what Jesus spoke to us, "I am with you always, *even* to the end of the age" (Matthew 28:20). You're never alone. You will get through to the other side. You will overcome. God Almighty, is holding your hand.

Take it Easy, Just Believe

"Most assuredly, I say to you, he who believes in Me, the works that I do he will do also; and greater *works* than these he will do, because I go to My Father. And whatever you ask in My name, that I will do, that the Father may be glorified in the Son. If you ask anything in My name, I will do *it.* (John 14:12-14)

Sometimes we think that God is asking us to do the impossible and wants us to solve our problem ourselves. We think He wants us to just figure it all out—to get our act together. We think, maybe we just need to try harder. But that's not who God is. He's not asking you to do things He knows you can't do in your own strength.

Remember, His yoke is easy, His burden is light (Matthew 11:30). The only thing God wants us to do is simply believe in Him.

God is your helper. He can and does want to help you with the things you cannot accomplish on your own.

Notice what verse fourteen says: "I will do it." In other words, the problems you face will not be resolved by you, but by Him. Your hands are not big enough to deal with a God-sized problem. Your solutions—your deliverance—will come through belief.

Remember, as our lives go on, they should be simplifying. You can't get more simple than simply believing God will do what He says He will do. That's why God tells us to become as little children (Matthew 18:3). Children have no doubt in what their parents tell them. If a parent tells a child they came from a stork, they believe it. If they tell them that the gifts they got for Christmas came straight from Santa himself, they'll believe that, too. There's a simplicity in a child's thoughts. They listen to their parents—because parents know everything.

Let's apply the same thought process to our heavenly Father. God said He's not a man that He should lie (Numbers 23:19). He says His Word will never fail, will not return to Him void, that it would accomplish what He pleases (Isaiah 55:11). So why do we have so much trouble believing God will do what He said He would do, when He said He would do it? When He gives us His Word—

the answer to our problem—why do we brush it off simply because we don't believe it? We continue to struggle and suffer not because God hasn't given us our answer, but because we have elected not to believe what He has told us.

Think about it like this: once God gave you His Word, He gave you the victory to the God-sized problem that is in your way. You don't have to look anywhere else for your answer. His answer will work; it will not fail. Why? Because God gave Himself, since He is the Word (John 1:1), and God cannot fail.

What kind of response does this demand? Not doubt. Not fear. It must be belief.

In my own struggles, I have discovered that my victory didn't come by being angry, or by trying to make it happen in my own strength. My victory came through believing what God had said, and taking God for His Word. That doesn't mean things were easy. There were times I wanted to give up. There were times when I thought I couldn't take it anymore. But His Word sustained me. Belief changed my situation, turned the tables, and did what I thought was impossible.

This is further demonstrated in scripture in the story of Jairus and his daughter. For those unfamiliar with this verse, Jairus's beloved daughter is sick—she's going to die if Jesus doesn't see her—and he is attempting to persuade Jesus to his home. Jesus agrees to come, but it seems like he is too late. Here's what happens:

While He was still speaking, someone came from the ruler of the synagogue's *house,* saying to him, "Your daughter is dead. Do not trouble the Teacher." But when Jesus heard *it,* He answered him, saying, "Do not be afraid; only believe, and she will be made well." (Luke 8:49-50)

I love how all Jesus asked for was that Jairus "believe only." He didn't ask Jairus to resurrect his daughter, or to fix the situation in his own strength. He didn't ask him to panic. Jesus asked *only* for belief.

Some of you are in that kind of a situation now. Others tell you that it's over—there's no more hope. They say you should just give up and turn away. But because Jesus is on the scene, the opposite is true. It's not over; it's not the end. When you put your faith in Him, you will see the situation change. You will see God do something new—something you've never seen before.

Jesus shows us by appearing "late" that situations don't dictate when God is going to move. God does things in His time and in His way. Remember Lazarus (John 11:1-44)? Jesus waited two days to go see His friend. I believe Jesus knew Lazarus would be dead by the time He got there. So why did Jesus wait? Because He does things in His time and in His way.

Look again at the three men who got thrown in the furnace. God didn't send an angel to save them as they were standing on the platform to get thrown in. He didn't even stop the fire from being ignited. He showed up in His time, at the time when it looked like death was certain. He did the same thing for Daniel in the lion's den.

What am I trying to say? I'm saying nothing can stop God from doing the impossible—even if you think it's too late. God does His best work when it seems like the story has already been written. It means we have to believe what God has spoken to us, even when it looks like it's over.

Don't believe what your situation, or other people, tell you. We can't be influenced by anything or anyone other than God. Our greatest belief should never be in what we see or say, or what others see or say. Our greatest belief should always be in the power of God.

We must be in a constant state of belief that God will come through, even when the situation says otherwise. Even when it seems that God is late, or that He failed, we must continue to hold fast in our belief. He is your deliverer. He's your helper. He's holding your hand and He's going to come through for you. Don't be afraid when you run into seemingly impossible situations, or God-sized problems. Know that this situation is in your Father's hands and He will take care of it. Take it easy, and just believe.

Chapter 9: Perseverance

The Shadow of Death

Yea, though I walk through the valley of the shadow of death, I will fear no evil; for You *are* with me; Your rod and Your staff, they comfort me. (Psalm 23:4)

Life, is not easy. There will be times in our life where we feel like we can't go on. Things have been too dark or we've been struggling for too long. Maybe we feel like we're at the end of our rope and we can't go forward anymore. Friend, from someone who's been there, let me encourage you to keep moving forward. There is something good on the other side. It will all be worth it.

God never said our lives would be easy, or that there wouldn't be times of turmoil or confusion. In fact, scripture says that many are the afflictions of the righteous (Psalms 34:19). So if difficulty is to be expected, what should our response be when difficulties come? Is the appropriate response to run away? To curse God asking why we're going through what we're going through? Or maybe the answer is to give up? The answer is none of these. Our response must be to keep going through.

You can't run away from your problems. If you run away from your problems, your difficulties, you'll being running away from the good that God has in store for you. Often time, we'll go through hell, right before we get to heaven.

In this psalm above, notice how David sees the reality of the valley of the shadow of death. How does this apply to you? It means that it's not a matter of "if" we will go through the valley, but "when." This Christian life isn't all sunshine and rainbows. It will be painful. There are going to be some nasty things you will see and go through. However, God promises to be with us during every dark times we go through. He's not going to take you out of the dark times. Instead, He will take you through.

Sometimes we think that God is just going to take us out of our situation. We think that there is no way a Christian should suffer, feel pain, or be uncomfortable. No, we *will* go through times like these. Think about the things the apostles went through in the Bible. Why should we think that we won't experience some kind of suffering in our lives, too?

However, what we can hold onto is the fact that God is still going to be with us as a shepherd watches and guides His sheep. Even though we will go through dark times, those dark times will not defeat us. The valley—the darkness—won't last forever. You will get to the other side, but you need to keep moving forward in faith.

Keep Moving Forward

And Pharaoh said to his servants, "Can we find *such a one* as this, a man in whom *is* the Spirit of God?" Then Pharaoh said to Joseph, "Inasmuch as God has shown you all this, *there is* no one as discerning and wise as you. You shall be over my house, and all my people shall be ruled according to your word; only in regard to the throne will I be greater than you." And Pharaoh said to Joseph, "See, I have set you over all the land of Egypt." Then Pharaoh took his signet ring off his hand and put it on Joseph's hand; and he clothed him in garments of fine linen and put a gold chain around his neck. And he had him ride in the second chariot which he had; and they cried out before him, "Bow the knee!" So he set him over all the land of Egypt. Pharaoh also said to Joseph, "I *am* Pharaoh, and without your consent no man may lift his hand or foot in all the land of Egypt." (Genesis 41:38-44)

One clear example where we see the need to move forward is in the story of Joseph. Let's review his life. God gave Joseph a dream, a promise that he would rule one day. But soon after this dream, Joseph is sold into slavery by his own family. He comes into the service of Potiphar and rises through the ranks. Things start to look better for Joseph, but not for long. Potiphar's wife attempts to seduce Joseph, and he does the right thing, says no, and runs away from her, leaving her holding a piece of his garment. She proceeds to tell her husband that Joseph attempted to rape her. Potiphar naturally believes his wife over a Hebrew slave and Joseph is then thrown into jail for a crime he didn't commit. While in jail, Joseph interprets a dream for a baker and a wine tester. When the wine tester is restored to his prior position at Pharaoh's service, he forgets his promise to vouch for Joseph until Pharaoh has a troubling dream. The man then tells Pharaoh that Joseph could interpret his dream. After Joseph interprets the dream, he becomes the number two ruler in the greatest nation of the world.

So what do we see here? In all these things that Joseph went through, he kept on moving forward in faith. Even when the circumstances seemed dire, and that he was on the wrong path, Joseph chose to stick to his faith in God, and was rewarded for it. Turns out, God had him on the right path the whole time, even when it didn't look like it.

Imagine if Joseph had given up. What if he had decided that enough was finally enough? He had every right to think so based on what he saw on the outside. I mean, could he seriously have dreamed about ruling when he was a slave? Although he couldn't see his journey was being orchestrated by God, his faith kept him moving forward.

Now let's apply that to us.

Do you think you would keep moving forward in your faith if you had been faced with all Joseph endured? Maybe you feel as though so many bad things have happened in your life. You wonder how it's possible for one person to go through so many bad things. How is it possible for one person to get all the bad breaks? You question if things will ever turn around.

Let me tell you something to encourage you. Your situation will turn around in your favor.

There will be a season and a time when everything goes right for you. What you're going through is simply maturing you—preparing you—for where you're going to go. But you can't give up. You've come too far to turn around. You need to keep going forward, to persevere, in His strength.

You might be telling yourself, "I literally haven't done anything wrong. Why am I going through this? I mean I know I'm not perfect, and maybe I have made mistakes, but my heart is in God's hands. I've done my best for Him. What have I done to deserve this?"

Perhaps what you're going through, is God showing His favor to you. How so? Because, in order to get to the fulfillment of what has been promised, in order to go where you've never gone before, you need to go through things you've never gone through before. You may not be struggling, because you did something wrong. It could be God simply wants to do something special in your life, like how He did for Joseph. God has a plan—never doubt that.

So don't give up. Keep moving forward. I love what Rocky says in the movie *Rocky Balboa*. He says, "Life's not about how hard you can hit, but about how hard you can get hit, and keep moving forward, how much you can take, and keep moving forward. That's how winning is done." You win by moving forward. You don't win by turning around and running. In this journey, we are going to take hits. We are going to get hurt. There will be times when we are knocked down, when the referee is standing over our body counting to ten. But God can and will strengthen you during those times. He'll give you the strength to get up again, because what you've been praying for, what you've been waiting for, is on the other side.

We must progress through hell, to get to heaven, to the resolution, and the fulfillment of what God has promised you. The hell you may be going through won't last forever, and soon your life won't be filled with heartbreak and pain anymore, but with wholeness, gladness, and fulfillment. Once you reach that fulfillment—that resolution—it's going to be so good it'll wash away the memories of all the bad that has happened to you. There will be a day of fulfillment, a day of reimbursement. There will be a day when what has been promised, will be delivered. So keep moving forward. The promise is at hand.

It Will Be Worth It

And the LORD restored Job's losses when he prayed for his friends.

Indeed the LORD gave Job twice as much as he had before. Then all his brothers, all his sisters, and all those who had been his acquaintances before, came to him and ate food with him in his house; and they consoled him and comforted him for all the adversity that the LORD had brought upon him. Each one gave him a piece of silver and each a ring of gold. Now the LORD blessed the latter *days* of Job more than his beginning; for he had fourteen thousand sheep, six thousand camels, one thousand yoke of oxen, and one thousand female donkeys. He also had seven sons and three daughters. And he called the name of the first Jemimah, the name of the second Keziah, and the name of the third Keren-Happuch. In all the land were found no women *so* beautiful as the daughters of Job; and their father gave them an inheritance among their brothers. After this Job lived one hundred and forty years, and saw his children and grandchildren *for* four generations. So Job died, old and full of days. (Job 42:10-17)

All the pain you experienced on this journey will be worth it. There will be a resolution worthy of what you've gone through. Although it may have seemed like every time something could have gone right, it went wrong, there's going to be a time when every time the coin flips, it will be in your favor. Things will go right for you. God is going to give you double for your troubles. You didn't go through what you went through for nothing.

We see this demonstrated in the story of Job. Here's the condensed version of what happens: Job lived a righteous life before God. There was no one like him in all the earth. The devil sees this and says to God, "He's only doing right because you've blessed him so much. Let me mess with him, and he'll turn on you." God allows the devil to do so, because He knows that Job won't turn on Him. Job stays true to God, trial, after trial, after trial. Even when his wife tells him to curse God and die, he refuses to do so and stays true to God. This man cut his own sores with pieces of broken pottery, and still didn't curse God. All his children were taken from him and he still didn't curse God. His own friends told him he must have sinned, and still he didn't curse God. He stayed true to God—he persevered. And, in the end, look what God did for him. He blessed Job with more than he had lost. He restored him with double the blessings of before.

It may feel like you've gone through the same things. It may feel like nothing good has ever happened to you. Even though you feel like you've done nothing wrong, even though you're trying to live a righteous life. It may feel like you've lost everything, that you're in a constant state of pain, and it seems like there isn't going to be an end. Believe me when I tell you—there is going to be a time when everything you've lost will be nothing in comparison to what you've gained. God will restore what has been taken from you. He will bless you like you've never been blessed before. There will be a time of reimbursement, and it won't be what you lost, it'll be double, just like Job.

However, consider this: Before Job got all the good, he had to go through the bad and he had to keep moving forward. He continued to seek God's face when everyone around him encouraged him to turn from his faith.

The same applies to you. Stay true to God on this journey you're on. It may not always be pretty. You might be saying some things from a place of hurt, or doing things from a place of hurt, but keep going forward. I know it hurts. I know everything looks dark, and that your situation may look hopeless. But there is something greater on the other side of your suffering. If you keep moving forward, and keep your faith alive, everything you've gone through will come to a glorious resolution. The valley won't compare to the mountaintop. Remember, even when it feels like God has abandoned you, He's been with you every step of the way.

Chapter 10: God of Time

His Seasons

To everything *there is* a season, A time for every purpose under heaven: A time to be born, And a time to die; A time to plant, And a time to pluck *what is* planted; A time to kill, And a time to heal; A time to break down, And a time to build up; A time to weep, And a time to laugh; A time to mourn, And a time to dance; A time to cast away stones, And a time to gather stones; A time to embrace, And a time to refrain from embracing; A time to gain, And a time to lose; A time to keep, And a time to throw away; A time to tear, And a time to sew; A time to keep silence, And a time to speak; A time to love, And a time to hate; A time of war, And a time of peace. (Ecclesiastes 3:1-8)

The God we serve is a God of seasons. We will go through seasons of joy, seasons of pain, seasons of life, and seasons of death. There is a season and a time for everything under the sun.

And no season will be exactly the same as the next. The seasons we go through vary as much as summer and winter. However, what is consistent is that the seasons we go through in life aren't regulated by time as we know it. They're regulated by truth and revelation.

You won't leave the season you're in until you learn what God is trying to teach you. You will stay there until there has been a change in your life. Every season has a purpose and there is a purpose to the season you are in. It may be a painful season. You might be suffering like never before, but God has you there for a reason. There is something necessary to your future in that season. God's seasons all happen on purpose. You will come out better on the other side.

Some seasons we go through serve as seasons of transition. Everything feels as though it's shifting and falling around you. Everything you thought you knew may feel like it's coming down. However, just because you're feeling shifts and shaking in your life, doesn't mean it's a bad thing. God allows these "earthquakes" in your life because of how much He loves you. He knows that everything that is contrary to your foundation—Jesus—falls away during these times. All this "shaking" works on your behalf. I love what Casting Crowns says in one of their songs entitled, "Just Be Held." It says "Your world's not falling apart, it's falling into place." When it looks like everything is falling down, it just means that God is trying to put your life in order. So when you feel unstable, know that He is stable, and His foundation will never collapse, it's as sure and true as God Himself.

So whatever season you may find yourself in, believe there is a reason why you are where you are. You wouldn't be there unless God allowed it. I know earthquakes may be scary, and you may be looking for something that's stable to hang on to. Hang on to His Word! Trust that even though you see everything falling down, when you stand on the Word, everything will fall into place. Once the dust settles, you'll see that all of it has worked to your good.

His Timing

While He was still speaking, someone came from the ruler of the synagogue's *house,* saying to him, "Your daughter is dead. Do not trouble the Teacher." But when Jesus heard *it,* He answered him, saying, "Do not be afraid; only believe, and she will be made well." When He came into the house, He permitted no one to go in except Peter, James, and John, and the father and mother of the girl. Now all wept and mourned for her; but He said, "Do not weep; she is not dead, but sleeping." And they ridiculed Him, knowing that she was dead. But He put them all outside, took her by the hand and called, saying, "Little girl, arise." Then her spirit returned, and she arose immediately. And He commanded that she be given *something* to eat. And her parents were astonished, but He charged them to tell no one what had happened. (Luke 8:49-56)

We've examined God's seasons, but what of His timing? Some of you may be wondering, "Where is God now?" You're struggling and it looks like God should have shown up a long time ago. We need to remember that God's timing is perfect. As the saying goes, "God always comes at 11:59." God always seems to come at the very last second, and sometimes it'll even look like God came through too late. However, we can always count on God to come at the *right* time.

As demonstrated in this passage of scripture, God is never too late. This is, again, the story of Jairus whose daughter was very sick, to the point of death. He ran to Jesus, knowing only Jesus could heal her. While Jesus was speaking with Jairus someone told them the daughter had died. It seemed like, now, Jesus was too late to heal

Jairus's daughter. It looked like Jesus, had made a mistake. But Jesus knew the outcome that others could not see.

The situation said that Jesus had failed. The situation said that Jesus couldn't come through in the clutch. The situation said that God was too late. And yet, everything worked out perfectly because God did something greater than what was originally expected. People expected a healing, but instead, were treated to a front row seat to a resurrection. They saw an impossible healing take place. Who do you think got the glory out of that? Not the situation, the doubt, or the fear. The situation tried to dictate that it was over, but here we see that no authority is greater than God's. Only God's authority matters.

Some of you are trapped in situations that you feel you cannot overcome. Maybe it feels like God has failed you. Maybe it seems too late. But that's a lie. We can't walk by what we simply see—we need to walk by faith. We need to walk by every Word of the living God. The power of God trespasses and overtakes the boundaries that we see, even life and death. It's greater than any situation. It's not over, until God says it's over. You will see the impossible take place. You will see your son or daughter come home. You will see that person you lost, recovered. You will see what looks dead, come to life. You will see that heartbreak you experienced, that you thought would never heal, be healed. God is going to take care of it. He's going to move. And He's going to do it in His perfect time.

You may not have experienced it yet, but it's coming. God said He would withhold no good thing from you (Psalm 84:11). God wants to do something greater than what you originally expected, just like He did with Jairus. He's the God that does above and beyond what we could ever imagine. Trust God's timing. He loves you too much to give you something out of His timing. He's looking out for you and He's going to do something great. Keep believing in what He said and watch what God will do.

Waiting on the Lord

But those who wait on the LORD Shall renew *their* strength; they shall mount up with wings like eagles, they shall run and not be weary, they shall walk and not faint. (Isaiah 40:31)

What does it mean to wait upon the Lord? Does it mean we're waiting with our hands neatly folded across our laps, tapping our toes as we wait for God? No. To wait upon God is to be in eager expectation believing He is going to do what He said He is going to do at the right time, at the right season. It means we've let go of our own efforts. We've let go of trying to make things happen ourselves, and we've left matters in the capable hands of the Father.

Many times we try so hard to make things happen. We try to make God do something when we want Him to do something. We want Him to work on *our* timetable. We try to be in control of every detail of our lives when our lives are not our own to begin with. We can't live on our timetable anymore. We must live on God's. Our timetables must align with God's. It's better that way.

When we try to make things happen on our own, we enter into a place of weakness. Why? Because we're relying on the strength of our own hand instead of God's for something that only God can do. Do you think Moses could have parted the sea in his own strength? Or called down the plagues on Egypt on his own? No. These could only be the works of the Almighty God. Moses believed that God would do what He said He would do. Moses was in a place of strength because He didn't rely on himself. He relied on God.

We need to be in a constant state of letting things go to God.

Jesus said that His yoke is easy, and that His burden is light (Matthew 11:30). That doesn't mean it's easy to let go. It doesn't mean it won't be a challenge. But it does mean that when you leave things in the Father's hands—when you wait upon the Lord—you will receive God's result, which is ultimately better than anything we could imagine.

So stay in your place of rest. Stay in your place of strength. How ironic is it, that strength is found in letting God be God and trusting Him, instead of simply trusting only yourself? We're taught that we need to rely on ourselves, and that we need to be strong, when, on the contrary, His strength is made perfect in weakness (2 Corinthians 12:9). We can't rely on ourselves anymore. We need to rely on Him. We need to trust His timing. We need to trust that He is going to do what He said He is going to do. We need to trust that the time we're in is just a time of transition, until we get to what God has promised. We need to trust that what we're going through right now, is simply preparing us for what's ahead.

What you've been praying for, waiting for, will happen. So keep that eager expectation on God. It may not be as soon as we want, but it will be at the perfect time—God's time. Remember, God has a perfect track record. Even if the hardest thing in the world is to wait, do it. It'll be worth it. God is the God of seasons and time, and He has a season and time for you. Wait on God's timetable, and you'll see Him do something that exceeds your expectations. Enjoy where you are right now. What God wants to give you will happen, but you need to wait on Him. You need to have that eager expectation and watch what God will do for you.

Chapter 11: Light of the World

He is the Source

Then Jesus spoke to them again, saying, "I am the light of the world. He who follows Me shall not walk in darkness, but have the light of life." (John 8:12)

Jesus is the light of the world. All illumination comes from Him. He is the source of all light. He is the only light. There is no darkness within Him.

Sometimes we think that maybe God is not all good. We think, maybe, there are parts of Him that are mean or harmful. We think, "Maybe He really is mad at me. Maybe He does want to harm me. Maybe God is not all good."

But that's not who God is. Not according to scripture. There's no darkness within Him. He is nothing but light. He's kind, loving, and good. He's for you, not against you. He saw that we were living in sin, were living in darkness. So He sent His Son so that you and I don't have to live in darkness. We can live in His light.

When God sent His Son, He didn't send just any light. When He sent His Son, He sent the source of light into the world. This was no imitation. He sent *the* light. The *only* light. The only light that has the capacity to destroy and expose all darkness because it is the ultimate light—God Himself.

So when we talk about darkness, what are we talking about? Darkness is the absence of light. The darkness we see in the world is the result of an absence of Jesus. It's not that God isn't doing His job. It's not that God has walked away from us. It's that many have walked away from Him. And those who aren't with God, are living in darkness.

We can't blame God for the wrong things that happen in this world. It's not His fault. The world is dark because it hasn't accepted the light. We blame God when we're the ones who have walked away—not Him.

You see, we have a choice if we want to accept the light source or not. God will never violate our free will. He's not going to force anyone out of darkness. It's a choice we have to make in our lives. It's a decision that God has left in our hands. We have to ask ourselves what our decision will be. Do we want to continue to walk in darkness? Or do we want the light of His truth?

Shine

You are the light of the world. A city that is set on a hill cannot be hidden. Nor do they light a lamp and put it under a basket, but on a lampstand, and it gives light to all *who are* in the house. Let your light so shine before men, that they may see your good works and glorify your Father in heaven. (Matthew 5:14-16)

God did not leave this world without light when His Son went back to the Father. We are the visual representation of God in the world. Now that same light of Jesus, is living, and shining inside of you. You are the light of the world. You shine where no one else shines.

It doesn't matter if you've made mistakes. It doesn't matter if you've done wrong. God's Word is not dependent on you. When He speaks something, He speaks it into existence. Because He has said you are the light of the world, you are. It's not because you're a good person, it's not because you always do the right thing, it's because of what He said. You are the light of the world when you accept the light into your own life.

This doesn't mean that dark things won't happen in your life, or that you'll instantly be perfect. But what it does mean is that the darkness that comes on the outside, will never be great enough to overcome the light on the inside. And you can keep shining your light even if you're not perfect. You can still be an example of who God is, because of what God has spoken.

So since it's already been spoken, we don't have to talk like we're holy. We don't have to try to act like we're righteous. We can simply just shine with the knowledge of God's light within us. Think about this: a lamp doesn't shout out to the world that it's a light—it just shines. It just is.

We put too much focus on doing "Christian" things, and saying "Christian" words, instead of just being God's light in the world. We can't convince people we're Christians simply because we spend so much time talking about Christian things. They'll know when we shine the light of Jesus that burns inside of us.

You see, being a light isn't an action, it's a state of being. The good works that come from being a light are a result of the light that's already shining bright within you. It's natural. How do we apply this to ourselves? We don't have to be fake. We don't have to speak in Christian clichés. We don't have to pretend to be religious. We can just be. It's time for that same light that shined in Jesus, to shine in our own lives naturally. Not from our mouth, but from our actions.

When we have the love of God in our hearts—the light shines naturally from within and spreads to everyone we encounter. We naturally want to do good things, love one another, and extend compassion and grace. When we do that, people will see the light of God in our lives.

People are sick of hearing preaching—they want to see action. The time for talk is over. What people need to see now is a demonstration of God's love in action. It's time for the light that's within us to be released. This light can't be put under a cover anymore. It needs to illuminate and cast away the darkness. That's why we've been sent into the world. To illuminate the places where there is darkness and show the world the light of God.

Maybe you're in a place where people don't know who God really is—a place of darkness. Maybe the people surrounding you have never seen His light. They need to see it. God sent you to where you are because He wants those people to see the light that's living inside of you—the direct representation of Him. God wants them to come to the light, too. Remember God's heart is that not any would perish (2 Peter 3:9).

That doesn't mean everyone is going to like it. That doesn't mean people are going to accept this light. Some people prefer the dark for a time. As a matter of fact, people might reject you just like they rejected Jesus. They might mock you like they mocked Jesus. They're definitely going to treat you like they treated Jesus. Scripture says that a servant is not greater than his master (John 15:20).

In other words, how people reacted to the source, Jesus, is how they're going to respond to the light that shines from us. But regardless of their reactions, we need to keep shining God's light just as Jesus did.

Someone who has been drawn to the light of the Father (John 6:44) needs to see a demonstration of the light of God in you. They need to see how you love someone who has done wrong to you. They need to see how you forgive. They need to see you demonstrating kindness, and integrity in the love of Jesus. They need to see you take care of the homeless, and feed those who are hungry. They need to see that joy and love you bring wherever you go. They need to see God's goodness demonstrated in your life.

God knew what He was doing when He sent you into a dark place. He saw that person, or people, who could be saved, touched, and loved by the light of God in your life.

But how will they see Him if we cover up our light?

How will people see God if all they hear is lip service, and not demonstration? Jesus backed up everything He said with demonstration. We need to that as well. The only demonstration of light someone might see in this world, the only visual representation of Jesus they encounter, might be you. Our light needs to shine like a raging fire, not like a little light. And as surely as fire draws people in, so people will be drawn in when they see our lights shining for God. People will be drawn to His goodness, light, and grace.

So don't stop shining that light. Shine when it's difficult. Shine when people reject you, hurt you, and even say all kinds of evil against you falsely, because of Him (Matthew 5:11). Don't stop! Someone in your life needs to see that light. You are where you are on purpose. Stop talking and start doing. It's time to follow Jesus' footsteps and walk the same walk that He did.

The Purpose of Light

For God so loved the world that He gave His only begotten Son, that whoever believes in Him should not perish but have everlasting life. For God did not send His Son into the world to condemn the world, but that the world through Him might be saved. He who believes in Him is not condemned; but he who does not believe is condemned already, because he has not believed in the name of the only begotten Son of God. And this is the condemnation, that the light has come into the world, and men loved darkness rather than light, because their deeds were evil. For everyone practicing evil hates the light and does not come to the light, lest his deeds should be exposed. But he who does the truth comes to the light, that his deeds may be clearly seen, that they have been done in God." (John 3:16-21)

We've shown who is the source of light, as well as the fact that we're the light of the world. But what's the purpose? What does light do? The Light of God exposes everyone's need for God in their lives. The intention of light is not to shame or condemn, but to save. It's an expression of God's love.

The heart of the John 3:16 scripture, the heart of God, is about salvation. God wants you to live free from darkness in your life. He wants you to live free from the sin that's held you for so long. He wants to give you the light of life—a life of abundance. He's not trying to expose you and make you feel bad about yourself by shining His light on you. He wants to bring you joy and into a right relationship with Him. Light is good. Why do you think light is expressed right after the greatest known scripture of love? God sent the Light of the world, because He loves you.

When you start walking in the light from God, others will see that they don't have to walk in darkness anymore, either. They will see that by choosing God, they, too, can walk in the goodness of His light.

Remember, you can't make that decision for someone. Each person must choose the light for themselves. When God sent His Son, He sent us a choice. We can walk in God's light regardless of past mistakes, and failures, or we can continue in darkness. The opportunity exists—it isn't exclusive, but it also isn't mandatory. As good as it is to live in God's light, He'll never force anyone to walk in the goodness of His light. He loves us too much to ever violate our free will. This is a choice we each have to make on our own. What you choose, will impact your life forever. What will you choose?

If you choose the light, then that same heart, light, and grace needs to be demonstrated in your life. We can't shine the light of

God with the intention of hurting people. We can't keep trying to make people feel bad so they will do right. There has to be mercy, love, and grace behind every light we shine, and every dark thing that is exposed. Shining God's light will naturally expose people's need for salvation, but the light of God should never hurt anyone. We don't have to do anything but be who God created us to be—let Him do the rest.

So let's follow the example of Jesus and shine our light. Let's take on the same heart of the Father, and demonstrate what a child of light is. If we expose, let us expose the need for God in others' lives. If we want to demonstrate we are the light of the world like Jesus said, then let's do so in action and use words only if necessary. If we're going to be ambassadors for Christ (2 Corinthians 5:20), let's demonstrate who God really is—a God full of light, mercy, love, and grace.

Chapter 12: The God of Faith

What's Within

Now faith is the substance of things hoped for, the evidence of things not seen. (Hebrews 11:1)

God is a god of faith, and there are some things we need to learn about faith so we can get a clearer picture of who He is and what He responds to. To begin, faith isn't just believing that something is going to happen. Faith is the very evidence of what you are hoping for, it's that knowing that you just can't let go of. It's the reality that hasn't shown up in the natural yet. It's the essence of what you've been praying for.

We often fall into the trap of living by only what we can see. For example, our bills are too high, that person we loved is long gone, or our dreams seem dead. But we can't walk by sight. What we see with our eyes in the natural is not indicative of how things really are, or how they are going to be. That's why we walk by the Spirit, by faith. After all, we aren't natural beings, but, rather, have been born of the Spirit (John 3:5-8). This means that we don't live by only what we see with our eyes, we live by what's seen in the Spirit.

Let's examine Joseph again. Some of you might be in a situation like Joseph, where God gave you a promise, and what's happening in your life is opposite of what's been promised. You may feel like a slave when God promised you'd rule. Don't give up faith! Remember the outcome of Joseph's ordeal? Remember the fulfillment? The dream that God placed within Joseph, came to pass, even when nothing in his life told him it would. He persevered in faith, every single day, even though there was no indication in the natural that what God said would come to pass. You can't live by what you see. You must walk by the faith within.

Let's look at another example in Abraham. Abraham was comfortable in his father's house, but God called Abraham to go somewhere unfamiliar. He didn't have to leave. But he left because he heard God and he believed God had better things in store for him. God didn't even tell Abraham where he was going! He simply said to go to, "a land that I will show you" (Genesis 12:1). There was no GPS, no map, no direction, but God gave Abraham His Word, and Abraham knew that was all he needed. He didn't know even a single step to take in any given direction, but he still moved based on his faith on God's Word. He stepped out in blind faith.

God promised he would make Abraham a father of many nations, and that many kings would come forth from his lineage (Genesis 17:3-6). And God came through on His Word. Abraham went on to be the "father of many nations." His descendants included Isaac, Jacob, Joseph, King David, and eventually, King of All, Jesus Christ. What a God we serve!

Are you living in faith today? What do you see in the supernatural that hasn't shown up in the natural yet? If you do walk by faith, you'll receive what God said He would give you. You'll see Him do what He said He would do. If He did it for Joseph, for Abraham, for David, and for so many others, imagine what He's going to do for you.

Receive By Faith

Now a woman, having a flow of blood for twelve years, who had spent all her livelihood on physicians and could not be healed by any, came from behind and touched the border of His garment. And immediately her flow of blood stopped. And Jesus said, "Who touched Me?" When all denied it, Peter and those with him said,

"Master, the multitudes throng and press You, and You say, 'Who touched Me?' "But Jesus said, "Somebody touched Me, for I perceived power going out from Me." Now when the woman saw that she was not hidden, she came trembling; and falling down before Him, she declared to Him in the presence of all the people the reason she had touched Him and how she was healed immediately. And He said to her, "Daughter, be of good cheer; your faith has made you well. Go in peace." (Luke 8:43-48)

The woman in this scripture could have look at her situation and said, "This is impossible. Things are never going to get better. I need to just give up. It's been too long. There have been too many disappointments. I'm giving up." This woman spent twelve years in pain. She spent twelve years being constantly disappointed. But she knew when she saw Jesus that He would heal her.

She had faith in Him, and she knew that even though no one else could heal her, even though she'd been disappointed so many times before, she knew she wouldn't be disappointed with Him. She would not be disappointed with the Word of God (John 1:1). She knew all she needed was one touch. She just needed that one grasp of His garment. She knew that the answer to her unsolvable problem was in Him.

Look at Jesus' response to her faith: "Your faith has made you well. Go in peace." The result she was looking for was directly tied to her faith. That's what faith does. It does the impossible.

Let's look at another example in the story of the centurion.

Now when Jesus had entered Capernaum, a centurion came to Him, pleading with Him, saying, "Lord, my servant is lying at home paralyzed, dreadfully tormented." And Jesus said to him, "I will come and heal him." The centurion answered and said, "Lord, I am not worthy that You should come under my roof. But only speak a word, and my servant will be healed. For I also am a man under authority, having soldiers under me. And I say to this *one,* 'Go,' and he goes; and to another, 'Come,' and he comes; and to my servant, 'Do this,' and he does *it.* " When Jesus heard *it,* He marveled, and said to those who followed, "Assuredly, I say to you, I have not found such great faith, not even in Israel. Then Jesus said to the centurion, "Go your way; and as you have believed, *so* let it be done for you." And his servant was healed that same hour. (Matthew 8:5-10, 13)

The centurion knew that Jesus didn't actually have to enter his home for his servant to be healed. He knew all Jesus had to do was to send His word, and it would be accomplished. What faith!

What do we see in both examples? Faith activates the power of God to do what no man or anyone else could do. The woman knew that all she needed was a touch of His garment. The centurion knew that all they needed was His Word. What they both shared in common was that they had total faith in the King. Both of these people staked it all on God's Word, and they were both rewarded for it.

We need to apply this type of faith in our own lives. Instead of worrying that there isn't enough money to pay the bills every month, let's say, "Lord, my bank account says I'm broke, but I'm counting on you, because you said you would supply all of my needs." If our children are living in the darkness, let's say, "Lord, my children aren't walking the right path, but your Word says to raise them in the way they should go, and when they're old they'll never depart." When we're faced with sickness or disease, let's say, "God, I know what the doctor says, but You're the author of life, and You're my healer. By Your stripes, I am healed. Sickness is not greater than Your name."

That's the kind of faith that makes things happen. That's the kind of faith that makes the impossible, possible. That's the kind of faith that shifts the things that seemed to be poised against you, into things that are pointed in your favor. That's the kind of faith that will break strongholds, disease, and illness. That's the kind of faith necessary to live victorious lives.

You see, in order to get what you need, you need to act like you already have it. That's what faith is. Believe me when I tell you that there will be a time when it's not just "the substance of things hoped for," but will, instead, be reality. You will be healed. Your needs will be met. Your kids will come back. It will become your reality, just like it did with the woman and the centurion.

Have faith that God will do what He said He would do, and that even if all else has failed before, know that He won't fail you now. Staking it all on Jesus like the woman and the centurion did will make things happen in your life. Faith puts us in position to receive.

Faith Puts You in Position

Now the just shall live by faith; But if anyone draws back, My soul has no pleasure in him." (Hebrews 10:38)

The reason why this scripture says "the just shall live by faith" is because faith is a lifestyle. It's not just an action. It's not a one-time thing. It's something that we must do every single day. You see, you can choose to live a life in fear, or negativity, but if you want to see change occur in your life, you need to live by faith in God and in His Word. Living by faith puts you in position to receive everything that God wants you to receive.

For some of us, we turn and run at the first sign of opposition, when God told us to go in that direction in the first place. We become like the Israelites who were right at the promised land but chose to run away. We often run away, too, just when we're steps away from the fulfillment of God's promise. How can we expect to receive anything from God that way? How can we receive, when we're always running away? We put ourselves out of position when we do this.

But when we live by faith, we're constantly moving towards the fulfillment of God's promises. We're in a state of perpetual motion forward. When you run forward straight at your problems, equipped with the Word of God, you're running straight into God's fulfill-ments.

Let's use a relay race as an example. In a relay race, every runner has to reach back and receive the baton from the previous runner. How does this apply to our walk with God? Jesus, the One who came before us, is reaching out to give you something so you can continue your race. However, if you draw back your hand, how will you re-ceive the baton—God's blessings? You can't continue the race. You'll be unprepared because you haven't reached your hand out in faith to receive what Jesus has been trying to give you all along.

Sometimes we blame God for not doing His part, when in reality it's because we haven't done ours. We're all out of sorts because we haven't taken on the lifestyle of faith that God requires (Hebrews 11:6). We aren't in a position to succeed because we've taken our-selves out of position.

I love what Mark Cuban said as I watched him communicate with Skip Bayless and Steven A. Smith on ESPN's show, *First Take*. Mr. Cuban said that the goal of their defensive scheme when they went against LeBron James was to get LeBron out of position. They could not let LeBron be put in a position to succeed. The ball had to be out of his hands. The Dallas Mavericks realized that no matter how great a person might be, if they could get him out of position, they would minimize his effectiveness. The result? The Mavericks proceeded to win the NBA title—accomplishing their mission.

How can we apply this to ourselves? We minimize our own effectiveness by not putting ourselves in a position to succeed. We underachieve because we haven't lived by faith. We've let ourselves get out of position, or we've allowed others to get us out of position.

We need to stand firm in faith. We can't listen to what our situation says. We can't listen to what others say. They can't see the same thing that you see. They don't feel the promise that God has placed inside of you. Don't let anyone get you out of position. Stand firm.

Think about all the great people in the Bible. What if Noah listened to all the naysayers, all the people who said he was crazy for building an ark? What if Abraham didn't listen to God and never left home? What if the woman with the issue of blood, or the centurion, didn't have faith in God? Would the results still have been the same? Probably not.

They were able to do what God had called them to do. They were able to receive what God wanted them to receive because of their faith in God. They put themselves in a position to receive His blessings.

Faith puts you in position because faith will always lead to action.

Thus also faith by itself, if it does not have works, is dead. But someone will say, "You have faith, and I have works." Show me your faith without your works, and I will show you my faith by my works. (James 2:17-18)

Faith leads to action, and from that action, comes fulfillment. Action doesn't mean you make something happen on your own. It means you're depending on God to do what only He can do in accordance with the faith you have inside of you.

For some of you, action might be simply waiting on God. For others, it may be moving in accordance with what God has put in your heart to do. Your action might look different from someone else's, but that shouldn't stop you from exhibiting it.

If you put action behind what's within—if you live by faith—

you'll see the impossible come to pass in your life. Faith that is alive, will bring the unseen into the seen. It'll do the things that are impossible. It will do what you simply cannot. If you stake it all on Jesus, He's sure to never fail you. Your situation, will turn around. That lost person, will be recovered. Your needs will be met if we have faith that they will. God is the God of faith and you'll receive everything that He has for you by it.

Chapter 13: The God of Belief

You Must Believe

Now He could do no mighty work there, except that He laid His hands on a few sick people and healed *them.* And He marveled because of their unbelief. Then He went about the villages in a circuit, teaching. (Mark 6:5-6)

Belief is whatever you hold to be true inside your life. It's what's real to you. According to scripture, if you really want to see the hand of God do "mighty works," you first have to believe those works can be done.

Nothing in this world just happens. The same holds true for God. You can proclaim the Word of God all you want, but until you believe it, nothing will change. You'll still be in the same rut, still going through the same cycle, until you believe the word that God has spoken to you.

We need to be in a constant state of faith, and a constant state of belief. We need to take God for His word, and act like what He has said is true when everything and everyone else is telling us different. Remember, He's not a man that He should lie (Numbers 23:19). There is no reason not to believe Him.

Sometimes God has already given us the answer we've been looking for, but we keep looking for other answers because we're afraid to take God for His word. We're afraid to believe, because we're afraid God is going to fail us or that He's going to disappoint us. Let me tell you this, God has a perfect track record. In a world of lies and disappointments, we can count on Him to always be true, and we can always count on Him to come through. Let's take another look at the story of the ruler and his sick daughter.

While He was still speaking, *some* came from the ruler of the synagogue's *house* who said, "Your daughter is dead. Why trouble the Teacher any further?" As soon as Jesus heard the word that was spoken, He said to the ruler of the synagogue, "Do not be afraid; only believe." And He permitted no one to follow Him except Peter, James, and John the brother of James. Then He came to the house of the ruler of the synagogue, and saw a tumult and those who wept and wailed loudly. When He came in, He said to them, "Why make this

commotion and weep? The child is not dead, but sleeping."
And they ridiculed Him. But when He had put them all outside, He took the father and the mother of the child, and those
who were with Him, and entered where the child was lying.
Then He took the child by the hand, and said to her, "Talitha,
cumi," which is translated, "Little girl, I say to you, arise." Immediately the girl arose and walked, for she was twelve years
of age. And they were overcome with great amazement. But He
commanded them strictly that no one should know it, and said
that *something* should be given her to eat. (Mark 5:35-43)

We've already discussed that God cannot fail, even when it
looks like He has. What else do you see in this passage? We see that
belief is necessary to see the hand of God do mighty things in your
life. Those fears you may have, the ones that say God has failed you,
are wrong. As we see in this passage, it is impossible for God to not
come through. He cannot fail you. Believe that God can do the impossible and He'll do it.

It's easy to believe in God for the simple things. But can we believe God to deal with even the extremely tough situations? Even
the ones we deem impossible to overcome? Can we believe in Him

when others are ridiculing or mocking us for our belief? Can we believe even when the situation seems dead?

That's exactly what we need to do. That's what the father in this scripture did. Even when his daughter had died, he knew death had no power over God. When Jesus revived Lazarus from the dead, when He revived the ruler's daughter and when He rose from the dead, He proved it. And He'll prove it to you, if you believe. There is no barrier great enough to stop God from doing what He said He would do if you believe. No one can do what He can do. If you believe even when a situation seems impossible, you'll open the door for God to perform a resurrection in your life.

Some of you are in a different situation. Maybe you believe that God can perform miracles in almost everything, except that *one* thing. There's no way He could take you out of debt. There's no way He could bring home that child or loved one that walked away. He can't save this family member. But that thing you don't think He could resurrect or change is probably the thing He wants you to believe in Him for the most. He wants to work out that one thing. The thing that seems too big for your hands is what He wants to work out more than anything. He wants to show you it isn't too big for Him. Remember, all a God-sized problem means, is that it requires a God-sized solution.

154

But He needs you to believe that He can do it. Jesus couldn't do mighty works in Nazareth because of their unbelief. Will the problem be the same for you? Or will you choose to believe God for the impossible? Will you choose to believe that He can do what He said He would do? If so, you will see God do the impossible. He'll move what looked unmovable. He'll work out what you thought could not be worked out, and He'll do it all in a way that works for your good.

Ungodly Beliefs

For as he thinks in his heart, so *is* he. "Eat and drink!" he says to you, but his heart is not with you. (Proverbs 23:7)

Now that we've talked about belief, we need to ask ourselves, "What *do* I believe? Am I believing the *right* things?" Belief shapes our lives, and we need to make sure that what we believe aligns with what God says. A wrong, ungodly belief, will cause us to live below what God desires for us. It will cause us to live with our heads down, living in doubt and fear. If you're believing the wrong things, it may cause you to move *away* from God instead of toward Him.

What we believe deeply in our hearts is what motivates us to move in the directions we move. Think about the power of that. If we think in our hearts that we are unqualified, or that we are failures, that is all we will be. Not because that's what God said, but because it's what we believe. If we believe we're poor, we'll always be in debt. If we believe we're good for nothings, then that's what we'll be. These beliefs are wrong, and they hold us back from God's promises. We will forever be stuck in limbo, or always moving backward. God wants us to move *forward*.

Some of these beliefs may be deeply rooted inside of your heart for years, perhaps even a lifetime. But they need to be torn down. They've held you back for too long. We need to cast down every high thing that exalts itself against the knowledge of God, and bring into captivity every thought to the obedience of Christ (2 Corinthians 10:5).

That doesn't mean it's going to be easy (do you sense a pattern?), but the end result will be worth the cost. Instead of believing that you're worthless, you'll believe that you're valuable and precious in His eyes, enough so for Him to send His only Son to die for you. Instead of believing you're a victim, you'll believe you're "more than conquerors through Him who loved us" (Romans 8:37). What you go through as the word of God tears down that stronghold, will not be wasted. It may be a constant battlefield in your mind, but because the word of God is on your side, and is greater than any ungodly belief, you already have the victory.

Even though God gives us promises and tells us how important we are to Him, those false thoughts within our hearts took years to build up—so don't expect them to go away overnight. It may even feel like warfare going on within your own body. It'll be a constant back and forth, and sometimes you won't know which way to go. That's because there's a constant warfare between an ungodly belief, and the truth, going on in your mind.

Fill your mind and heart with the promises of God's word each and every day, refute the negative thoughts you have built up in your heart and, soon, you will begin to feel the power of the truth in your life. Just believe the Word that God has given you and He'll take care of the rest. The light of God's Word, is greater than the darkness and your mind will be renewed by that light.

What God is building inside of you will be everlasting. Trust the process. Trust what God is doing. Let those ungodly beliefs and mindsets fall—you don't need them, and they're holding you back. You can't get to where God is taking you with an old state of mind. Let God renew your heart and mind to be more in line with His word and His will for your life.

Godly Beliefs and Their Importance

Say to them, 'As I live,' says the LORD, 'just as you have spoken in My hearing, so I will do to you: The carcasses of you who have complained against Me shall fall in this wilderness, all of you who were numbered, according to your entire number, from twenty years old and above. Except for Caleb the son of Jephunneh and Joshua the son of Nun, you shall by no means enter the land which I swore I would make you dwell in. But your little ones, whom you said would be victims, I will bring in, and they shall know the land which you have despised. But *as for* you, your carcasses shall fall in this wilderness. And your sons shall be shepherds in the wilderness forty years, and bear the brunt of your infidelity, until your carcasses are consumed in the wilderness. According to the number of the days in which you spied out the land, forty days, for each day you shall bear your guilt one year, *namely* forty years, and you shall know My rejection. I the LORD have spoken this; I will surely do so to all this evil congregation who are gathered together against Me. In this wilderness they shall be consumed, and there they shall die.'" (Numbers 14:28-35)

So how do we let godly beliefs, and not the lies, overrule our minds? We do so by believing God's word, and letting that word move us in the direction that God always intended for us.

Why is letting these godly thoughts rule our hearts so important? Well, we see the result of not having the right beliefs in the Israelites. The whole reason a portion of the Israelites didn't get into the promised land was because their minds believed the lies in their hearts. They were free from Egypt on the outside, but on the inside, they were still enslaved. Many of them missed out on God's promise because of their mindset. Instead of believing God's promises, and the word of Joshua and Caleb, they believed those speaking out in negativity and fear. Even though they had seen all the great miracles of God, they reverted back to their old way of thinking, time and time and again.

When Moses traveled up Mt. Sinai to speak to the Lord (also the same time when he received the Ten Commandments), the Israelites reverted back to Egypt in their minds and made a golden calf (Exodus 32). They went back to their old way of thinking simply because they thought God had deserted them. The lies they'd been taught in Egypt were more dominant in their mind than the new truths God had given them.

Even after seeing God do countless miracles in the wilderness—causing bread and meat to fall from the heavens, seeing a pillar of fire lead them by night, and a cloud by day—they couldn't see God actually delivering on His promise of giving them the promised land. They did not believe that God could come through on His word. It wasn't God holding them back from the promise, it was their own fears and unbelief. They were so stuck in their old beliefs; they couldn't transition into the new. They missed out on God's best, because they simply couldn't believe. How heartbreaking is it to go through such an extraordinary journey, seeing miracles every single day, for forty years, and still miss out because of your unbelief? If the Israelites had truly believed God's Word, letting it replace their fear and doubt with hope and assurance, they would have *all* made it to the promised land.

That's why godly beliefs are so important. We need to let go of those old beliefs that are making us travel around in the same circles. We need to believe what God has spoken. Until we do, we will simply stay in the same place.

How many times have we been like the Israelites, missing out on God's promise because we didn't believe His word? How many times have we chosen to stay in our old mindset, instead of transitioning into the new one that God is implanting in our hearts and minds? It's time to let go of those old mindsets. It's time to let God uproot ungodly beliefs, and believe every single word that He speaks to us. Believe the word that will change your situation, not the one that will keep you in the same place. It's time to stop living with our heads down. It's time to move forward as God wants us to do—He is a god of progression, not stagnation. You won't get to where God has promised you otherwise. It's time to let our minds be renewed by His word, so we can receive everything that God has promised. He wants to give you nothing but the best. Do not revert to the old mindsets. They are only keeping us from where God wants us to go—from our promised land.

Chapter 14: His Child

Being Childlike

And said, "Assuredly, I say to you, unless you are converted and become as little children, you will by no means enter the kingdom of heaven. (Matthew 18:3)

What does it mean in this passage to become like little children? Does God want us to act immaturely? Perhaps He wants us to pick our nose? Or pick on that boy or girl we may or may not have a crush on? No. God is looking for childlike simplicity.

We, as Christians, have a habit of making everything so complicated. We put up barriers of "rules" beyond what any person can attain. We make having a relationship with God sound so religious and pious—so *adult*. Some of us have put so much time and effort focusing on technical things—like trying to build the perfect sermon, or trying to pray using the biggest, most complicated words—that we forget that the most important thing is to simply know God

(Matthew 7:21-23). We've forgotten the importance of being child-like. Our lives shouldn't get more complicated as we continue our walk with God, they should get simpler. We're focused on the wrong things.

How can this be when Jesus clearly states in this scripture passage that unless we become as little children, we will, by no means, enter the kingdom of heaven? According to Jesus, it's not complicated. There's no need for us to try to be deep and spiritual. We don't have to pray prayers full of big words and high ideas. We don't have look pious all the time or act mature, looking down at others who don't. We can simply be who we are before God and we can speak plainly before our Father. We can find joy in knowing Him just as we did when we were children with our own parents.

As we get closer to God, our confusing and complicated lives should change into ones filled with more simplicity. Remember, scripture says that God is not the author of confusion, but of peace (1 Corinthians 14:33). Each and every day of our lives should be in the process of being more and more childlike—and more peaceful. How good is it to know that our lives don't have to be complicated anymore? Our lives can be as simple as when we were children.

For example, just as a child relies on their parents for everything, we can rely on our heavenly Father. We don't have to worry about fixing our own problems. Just as a newborn cries out to its parents, we can cry out to God whenever there's a problem. We can leave it in our Father's hands and He'll take care of it, no matter how big or small it might be. God cares about everything in our lives so we can have that same absolute childlike belief a child has in their parents. We can have absolute certainty that our Father is going to take care of all of our problems. We can have absolute trust in Him and His word and He won't disappoint us.

Do you know how a parent can always tell when something is bothering their child? So it is with our heavenly Father. He knows when something is bothering us—we can't hide it from Him. We can be real and simply talk to Him about it. Not only with pious words or necessarily on our knees, but by simply pouring out our heart to Him wherever we are. God is open to hear us whenever, wherever we might be.

Will you take the things bothering you out of your own hands? Will you accept the simplicity of having your Father take care of you, instead of you always taking care of yourself? Can you be real and honest with Him? Can you be as exposed as a newborn before God? That's what He wants. He wants your life to be simple. He's your Father. Rely on Him. Trust Him. Know Him.

Knowing Abba Father

For you did not receive the spirit of bondage again to fear, but you received the Spirit of adoption by whom we cry out, "Abba, Father." (Romans 8:15)

Of all the ways scripture could have described "Father," scripture uses the word "Abba," which means "Daddy." Why? Scripture specifically uses the word Abba to signify the type of relationship we are supposed to have with God. He doesn't want to be a distant or absent father. He wants to have an intimate relationship with you.

Throughout scripture we see that God has always desired relationship with us, from Adam all the way to present day. He wants us to be close to Him. But we haven't drawn close to Him. We've been distant. We must ask ourselves, what holds us back from having that intimate connection with our Father?

For some, it may be fear. Maybe you're afraid you see what no one else sees—the deep, dark thoughts you have inside yourself. You think there's no way God could be happy with you, with those thoughts. You feel that the best course of action is to run away from

Him.

But that's wrong. God doesn't want you to run away. He's madly in love with you. He's seen all those things in your heart. He knows those dark things you think. And He sees all the good and bad about you, too. None of it changes how much your Abba Father loves you. Nothing will ever change that. We have no reason to fear our Father. Fear will only drive us away from God. He has come to break that stronghold of fear so nothing will be in the way of having relationship with Him. God wants us to have that intimate relationship with Him that Jesus prayed for in the garden of Gethsemane. He prayed we would be one with Him, just as Jesus was and is (John 17:21). He wants you to know that nothing will ever change the fact that you are His.

This concept is further shown when the scripture goes on to say that we have now received "the Spirit of adoption." God doesn't see us as outcasts or rejects. He doesn't see us as mistakes. He sees us as His own family. Even if our natural parents have left us, He never will (Psalms 27:10).

There's no reason to not come into relationship with our Father. As you come into that relationship with Him, you'll begin to see for yourself how much He loves you. You'll see for yourself what it truly means when people say, "God loves you." You'll see that He loves and understands you like no one else can. You'll see that there is no reason to hide in the first place. He wants to give you all the desires He's put in your heart.

You'll see that you are His world, and that out of all the billions of people on the earth, there's only one just like you. He made you unique and you are special to Him. You are more precious than a diamond. He will be there to wipe away every tear. He will always love you. He just wants you to know who He really is. Will you allow that to happen?

Forever His

But as many as received Him, to them He gave the right to become children of God, to those who believe in His name: (John 1:12)

You want to know what's so wonderful about being His child? All it takes is the ultimate simplicity. If you receive Him, believe in His name, you are forever His. It's as simple as that.

What I love about God is that even after seeing all the bad things about us, He still wanted us for His own. Regardless of whatever shortcomings we may have, regardless of the things we may have done, He still wants to extend the invitation for us to become His family.

Some of us know what it's like to be rejected or seen as an outcast, but God has accepted each of us just as we are. In exchange for your rags of sin, He has given you the robe of a king (Revelation 5:10). Now we have royal blood running through our veins, and we are no longer slaves (except to righteousness, see Romans 6:18). We are His sons and daughters. We have an inheritance inside of Him. We've been totally and completely accepted.

And don't let anyone tell you otherwise. Some people may look at you and say, "There's no way you're a child of God. I know you. I know your past. I know who you really are." But we can't let anyone's voice be greater than God's in our lives. Their words are contrary to what the Lord tells us. The truth is none of us qualify to be His, but, by belief, we are.

Maybe you're questioning it yourself. You see yourself and you think there is no love great enough to reach you where you are. You're too messed up. Remember what we've discussed: There is no distance the love of God can't reach.

Let's revisit this verse:

For I am persuaded that neither death nor life, nor angels nor principalities nor powers, nor things present nor things to come, nor height nor depth, nor any other created thing, shall be able to separate us from the love of God which is in Christ Jesus our Lord. (Romans 8:38-39)

Nothing you ever do will ever create distance in how much God loves you. Nothing you do could make Him disown you. Nothing in your past, nothing you do now, and nothing you do in the future can separate or change how much God loves you. Your sin can't do it. Your mistakes can't either. No matter how many times you've fallen or will fall, you're always going to be His. When God took you on, it was for keeps. He said He would never leave you nor forsake you. You're forever His. And all we need to do is believe.

Do you want to know how much He loves you? As far as Jesus'

hands extended on the cross. As far as the east is from the west (Psalm 103:12), going on into infinity. So stop worrying that God will leave you because you did something wrong. Stop being afraid that God is mad at you or that you're in trouble with Him.

Even if others may have left you, been upset and disappointed with you, God never will. He'll never leave you. And you can't let Him down, because you were never holding Him up. He's there to uphold you, not the other way around (Isaiah 41:13).

He wants to take care of the things that are too big for you. He wants that intimate relationship with you. But will you come? Will you choose to believe in Jesus? That God raised His Son from the dead? Will you profess that Jesus is Lord? He's been waiting for you. If you haven't, the door is open, and you are welcome. You don't have to wait anymore. Pray this prayer and let God into your heart.

Jesus, I confess with my mouth that You are Lord. There is no one like You, God. I believe that You raised Your one and only Son from the dead to atone for my sin. I pray You will come into my heart. In Jesus name, Amen.

Friend, if you've prayed that simple prayer, welcome into the family of God (Romans 10:9-10).

Chapter 15: Pursuit

I'm Not There Yet

Not that I have already attained, or am already perfected; but I press on, that I may lay hold of that for which Christ Jesus has also laid hold of me. Brethren, I do not count myself to have apprehended; but one thing *I do,* forgetting those things which are behind and reaching forward to those things which are ahead, I press toward the goal for the prize of the upward call of God in Christ Jesus. (Philippians 3:12-14)

Now, just because you have a new life, doesn't mean you won't make mistakes. You will fall. You may do things that are wrong. But because you have His grace, when you make mistakes—when you fall—you can get up, dust yourself off and keep moving forward. But don't push for perfection. No one is perfect except Him. Just keep moving forward. Keep pursuing God and His will.

Look at Paul, the writer of the above scripture passage. This man wrote over half of the New Testament. He survived being ship-wrecked and being bitten by a poisonous snake soon afterwards. He cast out demons in Christ's name. Any handkerchief or apron that touched him was taken to the sick so they could be healed. This same Paul is saying here that he hasn't reached perfection. And even though he knew he hadn't achieved perfection, his advice wasn't to focus on "getting there," but instead to keep pressing on towards Christ.

What does this tell us? It means to not wait until you "get there" to try to form a relationship with Christ. Start pressing on right where you are. The flaws, imperfections, and shortcomings that you see in yourself—the ones that discourage you—do not disqualify you from doing what God has called you to do. It does not disqualify you from having a relationship with Him. He wants to know you and use you right where you are. He says that you are the righteousness of God in Christ, and that you are justified for the work He's as-signed you to do. Not because you're perfect or qualified, but be-cause He called you (Romans 8:30). He's not expecting you to be perfect, or to live by your own righteousness. He wants you to live by His grace, as Paul did.

Sometimes we make our lives so difficult by trying to be "good enough" to do the work that God called us to do. That's not what

174

God is asking for. Paul didn't wait—he jumped right in! You see, grace doesn't just cover you when you make mistakes. Grace empowers you, and equips you, to do everything that God has called you to do. That's amazing grace. Grace meets you right where you are, and takes you to where God wants to take you. That's how good God is. I'm not there yet, you may not be there yet, but that shouldn't stop us from moving forward.

Leaving Things Behind

There's another crucial aspect of this scripture that needs to be said. Your past is over. Some of you are afraid of going forward because of the things that are behind you. Every time you try to press on, all you see is your past. You may be thinking your future is over because of that past. You might think you can forget about the dreams in your heart, and you can forget about God's promises because of the bad things in your past. Let me tell you something: Your past is not greater than your future. Your past, can't stop you from where God wants you to go. God has a plan for your life (Jeremiah 29:11), and He wants you to forget the things that are behind.

Everyone makes mistakes. So what if you may have made a few more than others? There's grace for you! There's mercy. There's love. You can't do anything about your past, but you can always press on towards your future. Leave that stuff behind you. It's important to know that your future is not affected by your mistakes. Why? Because your future is locked in, secure inside of Him (Jeremiah 29:11). There's no way you won't reach the future that God has secured for you unless you walk away. There's destiny for your life. There's a plan that God has laid out for your life that He wants for you.

But if you spend your time looking at your past, how will you see the good that God wants to do for you today? If you drive using only the rearview mirror to see, you'll crash. This is the same way you'll crash if you keep using your past to direct your future. Scripture says you must reach forward to those things that are ahead. But in order to reach and move forward, you have to start looking through your windshield. It's bigger than the rearview mirror for a reason. Your future is greater than anything that was in the past.

You can let go of your regret, shame, and guilt. God doesn't want you to hold on to them any longer. He wants to bless you. He wants you to exchange your sorrows for His blessings. He wants you to take on His yoke and burden, for it is easy, and light (Matthew

11:30).

Your past, mistakes and sins have been covered by the blood of the Lamb. When He looks at you, He doesn't see your sin. He's not looking at your mistakes. He's looking at the blood His Son shed for you. The blood that Jesus shed at the cross is greater than any sin. The price has been paid. Receive the sacrifice that has been made for you. Go forward to where God wants to take you. Don't be held up anymore.

Apprehending Christ

Now, our past is no longer an issue. You don't have to be perfect. There are no more valid excuses. So it's time to make a decision. Will we apprehend Christ like He has apprehended us? Will we disregard who we are, the right to ourselves, in pursuit of Him? We have to decide to be done chasing after our own desires. It's time to run after Him.

We've run after so many things in the past. Some of us have ran after men, or women. Some of us have chased financial gain and profit. Some of us have pursued power and position. Let me tell you one thing, the greatest pursuit you will ever have in your life is the pursuit of Christ. As you begin to chase after Him, God will take care of the things you used to chase after before. He will bring that special person to you. He will be your financial stability. He will be your source of power. When you chase after God, He will take care of you.

So stop chasing after other worldly things. You're looking in the wrong place for something only God can give. Don't live unsatisfied for another day.

The truth is, mankind has a hole in their heart that's looking for something greater, something higher. They try to find it in philosophy or religion, love for the wrong person, or maybe even science. I'm not saying these things are necessarily bad, but what I am saying is that sometimes we try to fill that hole we feel with things that cannot do the job. We're looking in the wrong places. That hole can only be filled satisfactorily with one thing: God.

You don't have to be one of those people searching for a solution to their "hole" problem anymore. God is here. His arms are open. There's an open invitation. God has a great plan for your life. But you'll never accomplish it chasing after other things. If you want to see God do great things in your life, you have to be chasing after Him. So run after Him. Chase after Him. Apprehend Him!

Seek after Him every day. Start the day off spending time with your Father. Read His word. Seek His will. Have a relationship with Him. Put Him first in your life, and let go of the desires of your flesh. Let Him come alive inside your heart.

Chapter 16: What Now?

What Have You Learned?

Therefore, if anyone *is* in Christ, *he is* a new creation; old things have passed away; behold, all things have become new. (2 Corinthians 5:17)

What can we do with all that we've learned? We need to let go of the old and start moving forward. We need to let go of ungodly beliefs. We need to let go of every past incorrect perception of God and embrace who scripture reveals Him to be. We can't hold onto things like fear to keep us "safe" anymore. We can't live being full of judgment and condemnation. Doing these things will only hold us back from God's potential for our lives. We must live a life that is dominated by His love and His grace. We must learn to trust God's timing and trust that He's guiding all of our steps. We can't live the way we used to. All things have now become new.

Many people seek a fresh start. They want a new beginning. A clean slate where their past can be erased. That's exactly what God's given you. We can live a life free from our past and free from the guilt of our mistakes. Because of what Jesus did on the cross for us, we can walk in the newness of life, in the glory of His holiness. He didn't have to do it, but because He did, we now have the power to become the righteousness of God in Him, to be the Father's child. Jesus committed the most uneven exchange of all time when He took our sin and shame upon Himself and gave us eternal life instead. He clothed us when we were naked. He loved us while we were still sinners. He laid down His life and picked it up again for you. All in the name of love.

From that place of love, we need to see that God loves us too much, gave us too much, for us to be living in anything less than His best for us. He loves you where you are, but He loves you too much to leave you there. He wants us to transition into something greater. He wants us to make it into the land that He promised for us. He doesn't want us to live on the outskirts of it, or not be able to claim it because of fear or unbelief. He wants to take us there and He will—if you're willing to let go of the old and take on the new.

Let's take on the correct perception of God, and how it applies to our lives. Let's love others, like how God loves us. Let's not judge. Let's not try to punish others for their sins. Let's lift up and embrace. When we see someone struggling, let's not gossip anymore. Let's intercede on their behalf. When someone is going through struggles, hardships and pain, let's not give Christian clichés and empty promises of hope. Instead, let's show God's love in action by taking on their struggles with them, understanding their hardships and giving real, honest and useful help with love and grace. Let's not do things to look good in front of man anymore, but, instead, let the primary motivation behind everything we do match our Father's love.

Let there be a change in the perception of what it means to be a Christian. If people don't want to come to Christ, don't let it be because we scared them away with religious antics. Put them in the best possible position to believe by shining your light and displaying who He is in the natural. Demonstrate the Christ being formed in you (Galatians 4:19). Let them see the new life that God has promised. Then let them make the decision. Let them be changed by the realness of God's love.

Stop making claims of eternal punishment, trying to scare people into God's kingdom. God never used fear so don't paint Him as the God that does. Let's, instead, proclaim His goodness and His grace. Let's proclaim how much He loves us and what He gave for us. The gospel is called the "good news" for a reason, because God is good (Psalms 34:8). Let's stop trying to paint ourselves as self-righteous, and just be genuine people. Let's bring Jesus back to the center of it all.

Let's forget who we *think* God is and let's see who God is for ourselves, from a place of relationship. Let's connect with Him. God restored relationship between Himself and mankind for a reason. He wants you to know Him deeply, intimately.

Some of you may not have that new life yet, but you feel God tugging on your heart. Know that the door is always open for you to come to Him. You just have to proclaim with your mouth that Jesus is Lord, and believe in your heart, that God raised Him from the dead, and you will have that direct access into relationship with Him (Romans 10:9).

New life has been promised to us. Will you live it? Will you drop the old? Will you believe in everything God says? If you do, you'll be walking in the newness of His life. You'll be walking the way He wanted you to all along. As I've said numerous times, it doesn't mean things in your life will be easy. Jesus said we would have trouble in this world. But He also said, "Be of good cheer, I have overcome the world" (John 16:33). The trouble you face will never outweigh the benefits of the direction your life is now going in. You're free from your past. You're free from how you used to live. God is moving you forward, taking you where you've never been before.

Where Do You Go From Here?

However, we must ask ourselves, where do I go from here?

For the unbeliever, there's a choice you have to make. Will you believe? Remember that God isn't the one who condemns us, but we ourselves are condemned by unbelief. However, you don't have to live condemned! There is salvation from condemnation. It's in Him. It's by belief. You have to ask yourself, what do you believe? Who do you profess to be Lord?

If you believe, then welcome to the family. Welcome to relationship with your Father. This is the best decision you've ever made. You now have new life inside of Him. All things have become new.

As you go on this journey of life, remember that Christianity isn't about you being absolutely perfect. Remember that it's not about you. It's all about Him. It's not about looking good in front of people. It's about His love for you, and giving that same love out.

Trust me, once you experience that love for yourself, you'll never be able to keep it in. It's so good, you'll have to share it.

You've entered into the best days of the rest of your life. God has a destiny for you. He has a journey He wants to take you on and a promised land in which for you to dwell.

For those of you who already believe, where do you go from here? Will you stay the same? Will you live a life of condemnation? Or of grace? Will you live a life of judgment? Or of mercy? Will you accept who scripture truly reveals God to be, and apply it to your own life? Will you lift up others like how He did? Will you see who this God is for yourself? Until you see who He really is, you're going to keep living a life of religious notions, and useless clichés. This Christian walk won't be real to you, unless you see who the real God is for yourself.

It's time to move on.

How Do You Move On?

I know it's easy to stay in the same place, holding on to the past, and never progressing. However, that's not who God is or wants us to be. God has always been the God of progression. If you think about the armor of God (Ephesians 6:11-18), you'll see that there is no armor for your back. It's because God has created us to move forward into Himself.

We learned about perseverance earlier. Now that God has taken care of everything that's behind us, we need to take that lesson of perseverance and strive forward. We need to be reaching and never stop striving for Him.

That doesn't mean it's going to be easy, remember? Life is going to hurt. However, even when everything hurts, especially when your heart and body are in pain, we must keep moving forward. You can't wait until all the conditions are right to move ahead, that's not real life. You have to keep moving forward, despite what's going on in your life. Remember what we talked about from Sylvester Stallone's *Rocky Balboa*. If we want to win, we have to take whatever hits come our way and keep moving forward. When you're in the deepest valley of your life, keep moving forward. When your situation or circumstance is telling you the opposite of what God's promised, keep moving forward. When the storm is raging around you, and the wind looks like it's going to overwhelm you, keep moving forward. Remember that Jesus is in the boat with you and that you were built with the storm in mind. Remember that the deepest valley is only indicative of how high you're going. Remember that the promise is greater than what you see. Don't give up. Do the best you can with what you have and move forward, God will take care of the rest. Keep going forward. Keep pressing towards God.

Some of you might still be saying, "You don't know what I'm going through. You don't know my hurt. You don't know my situation." Your life may look out of control, but remember when things look like they're out of your control, it just means it's under His. Your life is in His hands. He's with you every step of the way. He's sovereign and guiding your steps. He's taking care of you. So no matter where you are, or what situation you might find yourself in, you can keep going towards Christ, even if you have to crawl.

Remember that the same Jesus, that has overcome the world, is living inside of you. Your victory, is already within you. Whatever you're facing will be overcome. You're made in the image and likeness of your Father after all. There's nothing that can stop you, because there's nothing that can stop Him.

So it's time to move forward. It's time to let go of the past, to forget other people's judgment and condemnation. It's time to let go of judgment and condemnation in our own lives. It's time to remember the love that was demonstrated to you, to all of us, on the cross of Calvary. It's time to go on to where God wants to take you. It's not time to be held back anymore. It's time to see His goodness for yourself, to see the perfection of His timing. Experience the holding of His hand. You're going to have to persevere through dark times like Joseph and David did, but often we go through times like these because there's something good on the other side. But to get there, we need to let go of everything that's been holding us back, whether it be fear, ungodly beliefs, or unbelief. We need to move forward into Him. Believe in God. Have faith in God. He will come through for you in every situation you encounter in this journey, but you have to be willing to take it. You may not be where you want to be yet, but you don't have to, to get to where God wants to take you.

But we have to make a choice. God isn't going to force you into anything, and He's certainly not going to force you into relationship with Him. He's not going to force you to obey Him, and He's not going to force you to believe in the name of Jesus. God loves you too much to ever take away your free will. If you want this relationship with God, if you want to go on this adventure God wants to take you on, you need to believe in Jesus. You need to believe that He took our place on the cross, that He is the way, the truth, and the life.

You need to see who God is for yourself.

And as we begin to see who God really is, let's be real people before Him. Let's not be the Pharisee standing proudly, but the tax collector beating His chest. Let's focus on having our heart right before Him. Let's focus on loving others like He loves us. Let's stop fighting each other, and stand together in unity. Even if our theologies differ, we can be united by the love of God. That's what it's all about. That's what God is all about. It needs to be, what we're all about. That's how we need to move on. God bless.

Afterword

I'm sure that as I continue to write, no book will compare to the journey this book took me on. As I wrote and rewrote, I would always find something that ministered to me, that touched my heart. I guess I do have to taste the fruits first, before it can help others. I hope this book touched your heart and blessed your soul. I don't know everything, but I've tried to reveal everything that's been shown to me as to who God is so far.

My heart isn't to condemn those who aren't displaying God's love and grace. It isn't to make people feel bad about themselves. My heart is to show the body of Christ the things that scripture says are wrong, things I've seen happen too often in the church. There's a heart that wants to bring correction, not out of anger, but out of love.

We can do much better than what we often demonstrate. We can love each other in better ways. What good does it do for anyone if we ignore the main ingredient of who God is (His love)? That's what it's all about. Don't withhold it. Share it. Live it. Demonstrate it.

Embrace those who fall. Embrace those who are hurting. Don't simply give an "all things work for your good" rote answer to someone's who's hurting. Find a way to truly minister to them, instead. Weep with those who weep, rejoice with those who rejoice and stand with your brother and sister who needs someone to listen (Romans 12:15). Intercede on his or her behalf. Let's endeavor to demonstrate who God really is. Let's show the world that God is love. Don't let who God really is be a secret anymore.

About the Author

Samuel Angelito Mananquil has been a dedicated worker for Christ since he was a child. He's served as an usher, soundman, and youth leader for the Church—operating behind the scenes, and in front of them. He's continues to minister at other cities, while faithfully serving at the church God has planted him in, all as an ambassador for Christ.

To contact the author, email him at:

Samuel.Angelito.Mananquil@gmail.com

God bless!

Proof

Made in the USA
Columbia, SC
09 September 2017